TASK, TALK, AND TEXT IN THE OPERATING ROOM: A STUDY IN MEDICAL DISCOURSE

Catherine Johnson Pettinari

Volume XXXIII in the Series
ADVANCES IN DISCOURSE PROCESSES
Roy O. Freedle, Editor

ABLEX PUBLISHING COMPANY
Norwood, New Jersey

Printed in the United States of America

Library of Congress Cataloging-in-Publication Data

Pettinari, Catherine Johnson.
   Task, talk, and text in the operating room.

   (Advances in discourse processes ; v. 33)
   Originally presented as the author's thesis
(Ph. D. — University of Michigan, 1985) under the
title: Medical action into surgical test.
   Bibliography: p.
   Includes index.
   1. Communication in surgery.   2. Content analysis
(Communication).   3. Medical records.   4. Discourse
analysis.   I. Pettinari, Catherine Johnson. Medical
action into surgical text.   II. Title.   III. Series.
[DNLM: 1. Linguistics.   2. Medical Records.
WX 173 P511t]
RD17.3.P47   1988   617'.91   88–10396
ISBN 0-89391-459-2

Ablex Publishing Corporation
355 Chestnut Street
Norwood, New Jersey 07648

TABLE OF CONTENTS

LIST OF APPENDICES

Preface to the Series

Roy O. Freedle
Series Editor

This series of volumes provides a forum for the cross-fertilization of ideas from a diverse number of disciplines, all of which share a common interest in discourse—be it prose comprehension and recall, dialogue analysis, text grammar construction, computer simulation of natural language, cross-cultural comparisons of communicative competence or other related topics. The problems posed by multisentence contexts and the methods required to investigate them, while not always unique to discourse, are still sufficiently distinct as to benefit from the organized model of scientific interaction made possible by this series.

Scholars working in the discourse area from the perspective of sociolinguistics, psycholinguistics, ethnomethodology and the sociology of language, educational psychology (e.g., teacher-student interaction), the philosophy of language, computational linguistics, and related subareas are invited to submit manuscripts of monograph or book length to the series editor. Edited collections of original papers resulting from conferences will also be considered.

Vol. XXXIV. The Presence of Thought. Introspective Accounts of Reading and Writing. Marilyn S. Sternglass, 1988.

ACKNOWLEDGMENTS

I benefitted greatly from the assistance of members of my thesis committee in preparing the dissertation which formed the basis of this volume. The insights of my dissertation chairman, A. L. Becker, on the contextual influences on texts have been the major impact on much of my thinking in this project. I would also like to thank Susan Gass, Deborah Keller-Cohen, and Dwight Stevenson for providing careful and critical readings of each chapter. I appreciate Susan Gass's careful reading and insightful comments on all parts of the dissertation, Deborah Keller-Cohen's encouragement and comments on interpretation of data, and Dwight Stevenson's discussion of audience analysis and the use of texts in institutions. The dissertation would not have come into being without the generous support, encouragement, and critical comments of Richard Frankel. Richard Frankel helped me locate an ideal informant—a surgeon with concern and intuitions about language, texts, and learning to produce them. Frankel's research in language in medicine, as well as his years of practical experience in conducting research in institutional settings, has been most influential.

I also owe an intellectual debt to others who helped me at various points in my academic career. John Swales was an interested, encouraging, and critical reader of the manuscript. I appreciate his pointing out the relevance of research in the philosophy of science to my work. Between my collecting data and beginning to write the dissertation, a long conversation with Henry Widdowson helped clarify how I would organize it. I owe a great deal to people who taught me at earlier points: Larry Selinker, for insights about specialist informants and applied linguistics research; Russell Tomlin, for discussion of episodes as well as introducing me to discourse analysis; and Collette Craig, for introducing me to linguistic fieldwork. More recently, I appreciate the comments that Bonnie Mauch, R.R.A., gave on Chapter 1.

Personnel in the research site gave most generously of their time and professional expertise. Both the administration of the hospital and the medical school surgergy department were helpful in granting permission to conduct research in this new area. Because of confidentiality, they will be nameless. I appreciate the suggestions of the professor of surgery on how to carry out data collection, for suggesting problem areas for research, and for reading the manuscript. The residents gave of their extremely precious time to be interviewed, and I appreciate their seriousness, candor, good humor, and interest in this research. Secretarial personnel from both the hospital and the medical school were gracious in aiding me to determine which residents had assisted in operations in previous years. Because the reports were not cross indexed according to resident, it took a great deal of perseverence to locate the reports and the secretarial personnel were very generous and interested in the research. Personnel from the medical records department were helpful in locating the operative reports and in forwarding them to me, as well as in providing references and their point of view. I appreciate the help of the operating room nursing staff in their assistance in this research.

I appreciate the financial assistance provided by a Rackham Dissertation Grant, and a scholarship from the Center of Continuing Education of Women.

Finally, I could not havee completed this 2-year project without the support of family and friends. I am grateful to my parents, Rod Johnson and Gerry Johnson, as well as Tony Pettinari, Bianca Pettinari, Jim Pettinari, Pat Rounds, and Charley Basham. Tony Pettinari got me started writing on many mornings. The wisdom, good cheer, and constant support of my husband, Larry Selinker, has been unmeasurable.

PREFACE

Before studying linguistics, I worked as a medical record administrator. My B.A. degree is in medical record administration, and I worked in this capacity in both hospitals and in medical record technology teaching programs. When I worked in these positions at that time, I often viewed medical records as physical entities in a system. Some were heavier than others; some were more complicated to assign disease and operation codes to than others; some were completed and signed more rapidly by physicians than were others; some were little used for a length of time, and so were either microfilmed or sent to a more remote storage area, depending on the hospital where I was working. A few were subpoenaed to court; others were examined in research studies. And from time to time, one would get lost and we would have to track it down.

The director of my B.A. program, Sister Loretta Sheehan, O.S.B., sent us students to all areas of the hospital, such as the labs, patient care areas, morgue, and operating room, to observe how medical records are constructed and used. As I complete this volume, I appreciate the wisdom of this decision.

When I began this study, my viewpoint on medical records, in light of my linguistic research, had changed from seeing records as entities in a system to textual data to be analyzed. Prior to the study, I had done discourse analysis research which examined grammatical alternations in operative reports, and had also contrasted rhetorical differences in operative reports produced by native speaking English surgeons and by nonnative speaking surgeons. After doing these studies, "bottom-up studies, if you will, of the grammatical structure of these reports, I knew that, although I was working with an informant, a closer examination of the context in which these reports were produced could yield a more insightful description of their textual organization. I knew, as well, that the contrastive study did not take into account the level of training of the nonnative speaker (a resident) and the native speakers (more experienced surgeons). At the same time, I was studying discourse analysis with Pete Becker, and became influenced by his view of a particular text as an entity which is shaped by the context in which it is produced and, in turn, the text shapes that context. This view called for a broader examination of this particular text in its institutional setting. I was also, at that time, becoming familiar with the research of Rich Frankel, who, working in in an institutional setting, had a research interest and a sensitivity to the complex relationship between medical documentation, the processes that create that documentation, and the outcomes of that documentation on the patient. Rich reminded me of a statement attributed to Lawrence Weed, a physician who has attempted to redesign medical records, "The medical record is not the *record* of medical practice, it *is* the medical practice." This observation seems to me to sum up the influence of the text on the context.

Having completed approximately 1 year in field work in the institutional setting in which medical records are produced, and having reflected on the data for an equivalent amount of time, my understanding of medical records has changed again. To me now, the medical record is a complex matrix of texts, each of whis created in a particular context with a particular audience and referent in mind. Each text is created by a particular author (or authors) with certain degrees of experience and pressures. Moreover, the actual way in which the texts are created and learned depends a great deal on the physical setting, the physical format of the particular report itself, and the particular professional area of expertise involved. In other words, my sense of the medical records has gone from a *thing* to a more fluid matrix of processes — probably what Sister Loretta was trying to get us to understand all along.

This study seeks to understand one of these texts on the medical record, the operative report, by a series of "thick descriptions" of the process of creating an operative report, of the narrative and episodic structure of one text, and of the change in reporting styles over the course of residency training. In so doing, I am also understanding the setting in which these texts are produced in its own terms. In other words, much of the literature examined is medical literature, and I try to give a sense of the setting in which these texts are created.

Interestingly enough, the profession of medical records administration seems to be changing towards a similar direction of examining the *content* of the medical record. In an issue of the *Journal of the American Medical Record Association,* the President of the association (Kloss 1985:15) stated, regarding its current clinical data management focus, that:

It too requires a concerted effort, but one which is much broader and more complex than simply improving the accuracy with which data is abstracted and coded. It will require a focus on the *content* (emphasis in original) of the medical records — its internal validity and consistency — as well as new ways of thinking about its adequacy and completeness.

A linguistic study such as this is one way to begin to gain such an understanding.

CHAPTER 1

THE CONTEXT OF OPERATIVE REPORTS

I was just thinking as I was walking over to the telephone that this is something that none of us ever talk about, doing dictation. You know, you don't *do* it. I guess everybody is - and I know I learned it on my *own*. I never asked anybody how to do it or anything like that. In fact, I was em*barr*assed to ask anybody initially because since nobody *told* us, I felt they assumed *we knew*. You know, I didn't want to, you know, ex*pose* my *ig*norance, you know, so I went and to my own way and found out how to, how to do it.

Fifth year resident

Learning to Dictate Operative Reports

It is common practice in a teaching hospital for the resident who assists in an operation to dictate the report of that operation. Dictating operative reports is but one of a number of new duties, experiences, and responsibilities that confront a new resident in surgery. Although dictating operative reports is not the highest priority in the beginning resident's inventory of skills to be mastered, its importance is well established. From a medicolegal point of view, a 1978 HEW/Industry study (Cooper 1978) examined 4,000 malpractice claims and determined that surgical error (over 50% of cases) was the most common allegation. In these cases, the operative report becomes an important piece of evidence. In the same study, one third of physicians involved in malpractice claims were found to be surgeons. As a result, a careful documentation of procedures followed in surgery is of prime importance. Similarly, an adequate description of findings encoun-

1

tered in surgery is crucial for further patient care. In a British study (Card, Sircus, & Smith 1979) of followup care in a gastrointestinal unit, surgical findings were determined to be one of the most important types of evidence recorded for follow-up care, second only to pathology findings. Descriptions of surgical findings are especially crucial in medical followup treatment for cancer (Bross, Priore, Shapiro, Stermole, & Anderson 1972). Chemotherapy protocols may be designed on the basis of the description of surgeons' observations of the affected area.

In most cases, of course, it is unlikely that a beginning resident would be involved in dictating the summary of an operation in which malpractice may be involved, or in dictating the report of complicated cancer surgery. In such situations, other members of the surgical team would be more likely to take responsibility for reporting on the operation. Surgical teams in all cases consist of a licensed surgeon with operating room privileges granted by the hospital, and, in complex cases in a teaching hospital, senior residents (residents in their fourth or fifth year of training) are generally in attendance, along with junior residents (in the first to third year of training) and medical students. For future patient care purposes and for medicologeal reasons, the attending surgeon or even the senior resident would be more likely to dictate the summary of the operation in these situations.

Despite the potential importance of these reports, very little formal or informal instruction is given on how to dictate operative reports. One reason may be because operative reports are dictated rather than handwritten. Handwritten reports are constructed in situations which lend themselves to informal teaching between personnel of different status, whereas dictation is done in more solitary surroundings. For example, following an operation I observed, a first year resident and a medical student took the patient into the Postanesthesia Recovery Room. There, at the nursing station, the medical student wrote the handwritten summary of the operation (see Appendix A) on the patient's progress notes, and the first year resident assisted him. (See also Morgan 1980:48 for a description of a similar situation in writing postoperative orders.)

Dictation, on the other hand, takes place in a more isolated environment. Because of the need for soundproofing, medical personnel usually dictate in booths or (as in the hospital I observed) in a quiet room off the surgeons' lounge. If another person is in this area, he or she is dictating as well, and appears not to be interruptable.

In these dictating areas, it is common practice for hospitals to post suggested "formats" for the types of reports (such as history and physical examinations, discharge summaries, and operative reports) to be dictated. These formats function, in a sense, to provide an outline, or guide, of how to construct the type of text. These formats differ in the extent of detail provided, however. The outlines of operative reports provided to the residents are, at least in the institution studied, more sketchy than those for discharge summaries. In particular, no information is specified to be included in the narrative part of the report (see Figure 1.).

During the time that I was gathering data in the hospital, however, the article "How to Dictate Operative Notes" (Stanley-Brown 1983) was posted in the Residency Training Office. This article, while it does provide examples of a "well constructed" operative report and of a "useless" report, and also points out the types of information to include in the operative findings, does not give any detail on what types of information should be included in the description of the procedure nor how that information should be structured. Moreover, this article was not posted close at hand to the dictating facilities.

In order to examine residents' experience in creating operative reports, in-depth interviews (Paget 1983) were conducted with four fifth-year, one third-year, and two first-year residents in surgery in a large midwestern medical school. Each interview lasted approximately 1 hour and was audiotaped.

A fifth-year resident noted the differences between the "formats" provided by the hospital on how to dictate discharge summaries and operative reports. (In this section, in many cases I shall let the residents' words speak for themselves. In this study, all names have been changed to maintain confidentiality.)

> They (the formats for how to dictate operative reports provided by the hospital) just tell you the things that *have* to be on there. OK? Those things have to be on it: the pre and postop, the name of the patient, the staff, the anesthetic. It's all got to be there. As far as the content, they don't say

---

This is Dr. _____ dictating an operative report
for Dr. (*STAFF*) on
Patient's name
Today's date
Patient's room
Social Security Number
Preoperative Diagnosis
Postoperative Diagnosis
Indications
Procedure

Figure 1.   Format Provided to Residents Describing How to Organize Operative Reports

anything. Now, there's other dictation, you know, like discharges and stuff. Now those are a little more explicit. On those cards they'll tell you the same stuff, the patient, the date of discharge. They say in the dictation (to) say what operations he had, what were his admitting labs, how did he go home, what his diet restrictions says, they give you a little more detail in what you need.

(Dr. Alvarez)

As a result of the isolation in which these reports are produced, surgical residents adopt a number of self-teaching strategies to learn how to dictate operative reports. One such strategy is to consult the format provided by the hospital as mentioned above. Most commonly, beginning residents will attempt to read operative reports that the other residents dictate, in order to gain some idea of the type of information to be included in the reports. This type of self instruction appears to be nonspecific in terms of the particular operative procedure, however. In other words, a resident will not necessarily seek out reports of an appendectomy, for example, but rather, will read any available previously dictated operative reports, in order to gain some idea of their format. These self-teaching strategies can be found in other fields and disciplines, as well. A Ph.D. candidate, confronted with learning how to write a dissertation proposal, may read some proposals from former students and use a similar format, despite different content of the proposals.

On occasion, a resident will use such a report as a model from which to dictate. A fifth year resident (Dr. Taylor) remembered being in a situation where, although he had had experience in dictating less complex cases, he needed a model on how to report on a more complex operation:

I remember having to dictate a radical neck dissection out at _____ that I didn't know what the heck how to begin. You know, a four hour operation. I was used to doing littly bitty cases and trying to remember all that was done. I just had no idea. I didn't know the operation well enough or anything so I went back to the floor again and pulled out a dictation of a radical neck that had been done before. You know, the guy (the resident) was fifth year and then I dictated *my* case from that.

(Dr. Taylor)

A resident may identify another resident as having good reporting skills. Dr. Taylor, for example, recalled reading the reports done by a member of his team whom he considered to have good reports. He indicates here some of the frustration that he experienced early in his training when approaching the reporting on a new type of case:

Dr. Taylor:	There was one of the other residents did *good* dictations. He was a year ahead of me—Dr. Drake. I would start reading his, you know, when they came back, particularly early on when you really didn't know what was going on . . .
CP:	You said that one guy had good dictation and then you looked at his once. How could you—what was good about that? About his dictations that struck you?
Dr. Taylor:	Well, he included all of the information that needed to *be* there.
CP:	How far along were you in training when you noticed this guy's reports.
Dr. Taylor:	Two months.
CP:	Oh, right in the beginning.
Dr. Taylor:	Early, yeah. Early on, yeah. Because you had to learn. I did for each operation, you know, it's kind of a new thing, if you do a bronchoscopy, for instance, for the first time, that's you put a tube down the nose and look in the—you know, how do you *describe* that? After you finish, how do you go back and dictate this so that someone would *know*? So again, you go back and you dig out a case to see what other residents said, and that's how you kinda draw out what to say. And I hadn't done many cases until then. I had only done a few burns cases. They're all skin grafts and that's nothing to that and at _____hospital, I didn't do much other than a few bronchoscopies. So after two months, I started my first real rotation and we were doing a lot of operating and there were all kinds of cases and I didn't know how to dictate most of them. So I would go to the charts that Drake had already done and looked to see his reports.
CP:	Why did you choose him particularly?
Dr. Taylor:	Well, number one, he was *there*, you know. Number two, and he was good. I was just discovering how good he was at that time. I never knew Drake really before that. By looking at his reports, I've learned how to do those cases right. He turned out to be one of the best guys who probably ever came through here, you know. He was young at that time, too. He had good—he did everything well, so that was how I got him.

It is important to note that the resident chosen as a model was only slightly more advanced in training than was Dr. Taylor at the time. Dr. Taylor stated that modeling reports of residents who were much more advanced in training would not be as helpful as modeling reports of residents at the same level of training. More senior residents would not be assisting at the same types of cases as would the junior residents.

There may be unforseen problems with utilizing reports of residents at a similar level of training as a model, however. As I show in Chapter 4, the content and structure of senior residents' reports tend to differ from those of more junior residents because the reports include more information relevant to both the procedure and findings. Dr. Taylor relates his rationale for examining reports of a resident at his same level of training:

CP: So did you look at his reports for — did you look at reports of other residents too at the same time? Do you remember this very clearly? I mean, did you look at other people's reports too and choose his as being the best or —

Dr. Taylor: No, I just did his because we were on the same team and I felt that he was — looking at him and looking at who else was around at our level, I didn't want to look at the other intern. I figured he was in the same boat as I was. And the other second year, it just wasn't convenient. We weren't following the same patients. Drake and I were following the same people so we were looking at the same charts and in the course of doing my work, it wasn't anything extra. I just, instead of looking at the labs and progress notes, I'd turn — I'd flip over and look at his dictation if that was in there. And also my senior resident too, but not so much him, because he was doing the big cases and I wasn't doing those. I didn't feel that — by the time I got to that point, I figured I'd know! (Laugh) I wasn't gonna be dictating any gastric resections like you said or anything like that at that time.

(Dr. Taylor)

In addition to reading reports of other residents, beginning residents may also read their own reports in order to critique them. As Dr. Alvarez notes:

Look at somebody elses' and see what it looked like? I can't remember if I did that or not. I may have. I'm sure I did. I'm sure I looked at some of the old ones. What I *can* remember is the first couple months was I just started dictating them. As they came back, I read most of them for a while. I quite somewhere in that first year reading them, there were so many. And it's kind of a wise thing to read them through. Geez, there are a lot of typographical errors and you don't realize what you said and how it sounded. But I can't remember specifically if I ever went and read something first. I just sat down and went through the operation again."

(Dr. Alvarez)

Junior residents had a clearer memory of what they did to report on operations in the beginning of their training than did the fifth year residents. Both the first and third year resident remembered one problem that the fifth year residents did not recall: being uncertain about anatomic details crucial to the report. The strategy that they used to cope with this situation was to consult textbooks prior to dictating. The first year resident (Dr. Oliver) describes this strategy and points out that not taking the extra effort to clarify the medical terminology would result in a poorer report:

> There's been times when I've had to go home after the operation, pull out my anatomy texts and my surgical texts and then come back and read through the dictation because there are certain things that I recognize and I could dictate if I knew the exact names and all that kind of thing. But there's times when I've had to (inaudible) before I've had to do the actual dictation, so it'd be easy enough to go ahead and dictate it and not be able to name things, but I don't think that that would make a very good report.
>
> (Dr. Oliver)

A third resident, Dr. Hill, who was later commended by a surgeon at one of the residency training sites for having particularly complete reports, related his frustration in doing a report for the first time. Although the operation itself was performed under the supervision of an attending surgeon, the reporting on the operation apparently was not, and there was difficulty in remembering the anatomic terminology:

> CP: Have you ever had any particular difficulty with doing the reports?
> Dr. Hill: Doing the operative reports? Absolutely!
> CP: Like the first time you've ever done a case, whether it's a simple amputation or whether it's a gallbladder, and feeling like I didn't know enough anatomy to dictate an accurate and adequate report. And so I would put off dictating for a few hours until I could quick look in an anatomy book, so I could get my terms as accurate as possible. I remember in July of my first year when I did my first, an amputation, it was. It was a terrible report! I made an incision here, and cut through mucsle and didn't name the muscle and didn't name the vessels that we were ligating. I think that's a poor report. I mean, it's an *adequate* one; there are only so many ways you can do an amputation, it just wasn't a (hell of a) good report.
>
> (Dr. Hill)

It is obvious, then, that residents do not begin their residency training with experience in producing this particular type of text, at least at this medical school. This medical school is not unusual, however. Stanley Brown (1983:109) notes that "no instruction in this minor skill is offered in most medical schools and the currently available surgical textbooks give little specific advice." It might seem likely, however, that, prior to residency training, medical students would have had experience in at least the rhetorical acts of describing procedures and findings (see Chapter 4 for a more complete discussion) in medical school I did not ask all residents interviewed whether they had had analogous experience in describing procedures and describing findings in medical school, but, of those that I asked, the opinions were mixed. In terms of describing procedures, the first year resident stated that, as a medical student, he did have to record notes of certain procedures in writing. These procedures were not, however, reported in as much detail as those in dictated operative reports. In terms of describing findings, however, Dr. Oliver stated that he had not had such experience:

CP: Did you get any sort of experience in medical school that would prepare you for it (dictating operative reports) at all?

Dr. Oliver: No, not at all because that was always the job of the residents to dictate the reports. Students never actually had to do that.

CP: Well, in your training was there anything that was somewhat analogous to this, like, you know, if you did dissection and

Dr. Oliver: Actually, no, because where I went to medical school we weren't allowed to dictate. Everything we did we had to write out and so really there was no training at all as far as that goes. And the only thing that I ever really did was to see old operative reports and try to copy that kind of format.

CP: Did you ever have to describe procedures when you did the writing at all?

Dr. Oliver: Yeah, those were really brief notes, though, sort of the same as the operative report but just more the final findings, kind of a written report. In other words, we wouldn't go through, you know, "We cut the skin with a #10 scalpel blade. All bleeders were controlled using electrocoagulation." All you just said, was, you know, "Patient under sterile conditions. A (Swan-Ganz) catheter was inserted." And that would really be about it. Or "a chest tube was inserted under local anesthesia." We wouldn't go through and describe what size chest tube would be used and what we would do as far as the hemostats.

CP: Yeah. Would that be for—what would you be doing that for?

Dr. Oliver: Really, where I went to school, the students did all the minor procedures like subclavian (lines), (inaudible) catheters, chest tubes, and things like that. And we were expected to put a written report on the chart. Saying that what we did would be analogous, I guess for those type of procedures, to the dictated report.

CP: Did you have any experience in describing what you saw?

Dr. Oliver: No, there was nothing at all like that.

CP: Was that ever part of your medical training at all?

Dr. Oliver: No, not at all.

It might be supposed that examining organs during cadaver dissection would provide an analogous experience to describing the organs observed during an operation. Dr. Taylor reports that this is not so:

CP: And you never—in medical school, you didn't have to describe things this way. Is that right? Like when you would do autopsies, not autopsies, but when you'd examine cadavers and things like that, you never had to write about—describe it in any way?

Dr. Taylor: All you did was try to remember the names of the structures. That was it because there was no real report to do upon your technique and how you dissected the structures. You just had to get them out and remember them, you know, get them out and remember what they are.

CP: mm hm, you didn't have to describe the conditions of the structures that you found or anything like that?

Dr. Taylor: They were usually not too *good*! All you needed to do was show— demonstrate—the structures and remember them in relationship to other structures, etcetera. That was all it was. No, we had *nothing* in medical school that was comparable to this.

(Dr. Taylor)

Dr. Taylor continues, and points out the differences between producing discharge summaries, one type of dictated medical record report with which he did have experience in medical school, and operative reports. An important difference in producing these two reports is that information to be reported in the discharge summary can be found in other places on the medical record whereas information to be reported in the operative report can not. (Card et al. 1979) also noted that much information from the operation is not recoverable from other sources, such as the patient, or from other reports on the medical record.) In other words, the resident must rely on memory for reporting on the operation.

Usually, I guess most senior students get some exposure to dictated discharge summaries, but a discharge summary is a lot *different* from an operative report. And you know, that's not too bad, you know. Half of the discharge summary is just repeating the history and physical exam and then the last part of it is just the hospital course: what tests were done and how the patient responded to the treatment, what treatment was used and what the outcome was, what was their disposition when they leave and what the plan for followup was. You know, and you just talk to the attending doctor. He plans to see the doctor in his office and you're writing the prescriptions so you know he's gonna be on these medications and it's not that bad. The OR report is a lot *different*, because you can't go and look at the chart and find out how to do it. You know, you just did it and now you gotta put it down. It's an important record, you know; there's no question about it. I don't think there's anything else — you know — procedure notes, a surgeon does them. I guess, cardiologists when they do catheterizations and a few others, but there's not too many doctors who have to do those.

(Dr. Taylor)

Another fifth year resident (Dr. Rose) also did not feel that medical school activities had provided him with experience in producing operative reports:

CP: One last question. When you were in medical school, or even in your early years, did you do any sort of description of procedures or descriptions of anatomic details or anything like that? Did you ever have to describe things, describe them in writing? Did you ever get any practice in doing that?

Dr. Hill: Anatomic details? No. Scientific reports, scientific papers? Yes, many.

CP: Would that sort of experience transfer over to —

Dr. Hill: I think so.

CP: Like for example, what comes to mind when you say scientific reports?

Dr. Hill: Some research that I did at the University of_____ . Research that I have done privately all through high school and college, projects that I have worked on. I was an English major (inaudible) and I don't know, I just developed my own style and I try to dictate my reports in that style. You know, it helps to organize and it helps to get across what I feel is important in a logical and, if you will, a scientific way. I guess people look at my writing and call it a scientific style. (Whether it is or not) even back when I was writing critical essays for my English classes.

CP: Do you think that you might be more sensitive to the writing and the dictating because of your background in English?

Dr. Hill: Much more. Much more.

In summary, then, surgical residents get little or no formal training in producing operative reports when they begin residency training. Because of the nature of the dictating process, obtaining informal help at the time of dictating reports appears to be problematic. It appears that this group of residents does not feel that the skill of describing procedures and findings is particularly emphasized in medical school, prior to their residency training. As a result, surgical residents adopt a number of self teaching strategies to learn how to produce these reports.

A Brief Description of Medical Records

A person who receives any sort of medical or dental care in the United States will have some written documentation of that, whether it is for a visit to a physician's or dentist's office, or care as an inpatient in a hospital or nursing home. Although this study is concerned primarily with the production of one particular kind of report, operative reports, it is important to remember that the operative report does not exist in isolation. It is a part of a body of written documentation created by a number of persons of differing professional backgrounds. Before a more specific discussion of the nature of operative reports, I discuss medical records as a whole. First, I briefly present standards that influence the form and content of the medical record; then I discuss the content of the medical record; and finally I indicate the purposes of the medical record.

Hospital-based health care services such as in-patient, outpatient, emergency, and home-care programs have more regulatory bodies which influence the form and content of their records than do physicians' offices. When a patient enters a hospital, he or she has a number of reports written or dictated about his or her condition by a variety of hospital personnel. The different forms on which these observations are recorded may vary somewhat from hospital to hospital. As a rule, each hospital medical staff has a mechanism by which each type of form to be used on the medical record is approved. These rules govern, then, the physical format of the various pieces of paper that comprise the patient's medical record.

Authorship of the medical record is governed by hospital regulations as well. Not anyone can write on the medical record. Hospital regulations restrict the privilege of recording on the medical record to certain professional groups. For example, in one hospital, occupational therapists have privileges to write on the medical record; recreational therapists do not (Raffel 1979).

The Joint Commission on Accreditation (JCAH) is a national hospital regulatory body whose standards have become incorporated into hospital law. Accreditation by the JCAH is a condition for funding by federal and state agencies, for residency and intern training programs, and for university teaching affiliate hospitals (Matte 1971). Consequently, the majority of hospitals in the United States aim to be accredited by the JCAH and to follow their standards. The JCAH sets standards for every major department of the hospital. Included in these are standards for medical records services. The discussion of hospital medical records in this chapter follows quite closely the most recent (Joint Commission on Accreditation of Hospitals 1987) standards. Charfoos (1974) and Huffman (1981) were also consulted for examples included in this section.

Although the JCAH does not recommend any particular forms to be on the medical record, certain types of information must be on the medical record. In addition, any written opinions that indicate medical judgment should be written or authenticated only by medical staff members, house staff members (interns and residents), or others who have been granted the privilege from the hospital administration. These opinions must be "authenticated" by a physician. In general, this term, commonly used by the JCAH, means that, while an examination may be performed by a house staff officer, the responsible physician with medical staff privileges must date and sign the form (Raffel 1979). The following information must be included in the medical record:

(1) Identification data. The patient's name, address, date of birth, next of kin, and a number to identify the patient must be part of the medical record.

(2) Medical history. The main reason for performing a medical history (2) and physical examination (3) is to establish a diagnosis of the patient's condition. This diagnosis forms the basis for the care and treatment of the patient (Huffman 1981). JCAH standards call for the prompt completion of this history upon admission. The medical history is to be completed either within the first 24 hours of the patient's hospital stay or within a week prior to admission in the physician's office, as long as a copy of this is included in the medical record. The medical history should include the "chief complaint," or the reason that the patient sought medical help.[1] Details of the present illness, along with past history, and family and social history, are also included. The history includes an inventory of the body systems. In order to obtain this information, the provider questions the patient about each major body system, such as the gastrointestinal system, and the musculoskeletal system.

(3) Report of of the physical examination. Like the medical history, a physical examination is also required to be performed within the first 24 hours of the patient's hospital stay, or within the physician's office a week prior to the patient's admission to the hospital, providing that the copy of the examination be placed on the medical record. Commonly, (2) and (3), the history and physical examinations, are combined in one form. A statement of conclusions that result from the admission history and physical examination and a plan of action for the patient's hospital stay are also included here.

(4) Diagnostic and therapeutic orders. Whenever an order is given by a physician, resident, or other practicioner with privileges to order treatment, that order must be included on the medical record. When the order is given

---

[1]See Beckman and Frankel (1984) for research on the extent to which patient' concerns are elicited in physicians' office visits.

verbally, the person who transcribes the order on to the patient's medical record must identify himself or herself by name and title.

(5) Evidence of appropriate informed consent.   Patients must give their consent in writing for procedures and treatment in accordance with hospital policy.

(6) Clinical observations.   Clinical observations are the observations and interpretations of the patient's condition by members of the medical staff and by other personnel granted permission to record on the medical record. Clinical observations are generally recorded on the following forms:

(6.1) Progress notes.   Notes of the course of the patient's disease are made by members of the medical staff. These notes chart the patient's chronological course during the hospital stay. Their purpose is to indicate any change in the patient's condition and to indicate the results of treatment. Certain procedures such as lumbar punctures, bone marrow aspiration, cardiac catheterization, etc. may be handwritten on the progress notes rather than dictated in an operative report. Other non-physician personnel may also be granted privileges to record on the progress notes. Such personnel includes dieticians, physical therapists, nurse anesthetists, social workers, and hospital chaplains.

(6.2) Consultations.   The attending physician may need another opinion from another specialist in the event that he or she is not satisfied with the patient's progress, or if he or she needs an opinion from a specialist outside his or her area of expertise. In this case, the physician requests a consultation. The consultant gives a written opinion that indicates that he or she examined the patient and the medical records.

(6.3) Nursing notes.   Nursing notes are similar to progress notes in that these notes chart the chronological progress of the patient throughout the hospital stay, with the difference that the nurses complete these notes according to their areas of expertise. Only physicians may give opinions requiring medical judgment.

(6.4) Postanesthesia recovery report.   When a patient arrives in the recovery room following surgery, the postanesthesia recovery report is completed during the stay in this area. According to the JCAH, the medical record information here should include the patient's level of consciousness upon arrival and departure of this unit. Also noted are the patient's vital signs (temperature, pulse, and respiration), and the status of surgical dressings, tubes, catheters, drains, and intravenous solutions.

(7) Reports of procedures, tests, and results.   Again, these must be authenticated. The medical record may also include reports from other institutions, as long as the institution is identified in the report.

(7.1) Operative report.   See the following section, What Operative Reports Are, for a complete discussion.

(7.2) Pathology reports, clinical laboratory reports, radiology and nuclear medicine examinations or treatment, anesthesia reports. Each of these reports provides a professional opinion about a specimen from the patient or is an observation about a part of the patient. The pathology report is the pathologist's description and findings of tissue removed during surgery (Wagner 1984). Clinical laboratory reports are the reports of laboratory tests such as blood tests, urinalyses, and the examination of other body products and fluids. Radiology reports are the results of x-rays or other examinations performed in the radiology department, and anesthesia reports are the reports of the patient's vital signs, premedication, and medication given by the Anesthesia Department during the course of surgery (Charfoos 1974). All of these reports should be filed in the medical record within 24 hours of completion.

(7.3) Organ donor reports. If an organ is obtained from a brain-wave-dead patient, there are some required items that must be on the donor's medical record. The date and time of brain-wave death must be recorded. The physician who determined the death should document the death. The way in which the organ was transferred, and the machine maintenance of the patient for the transplant, should be included along with an operative report. If a cadaver organ is removed, there should be an autopsy report which includes a description of how the organ was removed, prepared, or preserved.

(8) Conclusions at the end of hospitalization. When the patient is discharged from the hospital, information regarding the reason or reasons for admission, the principal and secondary diagnoses, and the summary of the patient's hospital stay must be included on the medical record. If the patient died and an autopsy was performed, an autopsy report would also be included in the medical record. It is important for the final diagnoses and operative procedures to be recorded using what is termed "acceptable disease and operation terminology" by the JCAH. In practice, this is usually according to ICD-9-CM (International Classification of Disease, 9th Revision, Clinical Modification) terminology. At present, 95% of hospitals in the U.S. utilize this classification to code final diagnoses and procedures for reimbursement by third party payors (Cofer 1985) and for hospital statistical purposes.

(8.1) Discharge summary. When the patient leaves the hospital, a clinical summary of his or her hospital course must be compiled. This summary includes the reason for hospitalization, significant findings, procedures performed, treatment given, the condition of the patient on discharge, and any recommendations for follow-up care.

As previously stated, operative reports are part of a larger document, the medical record. Some of the above texts on the medical record could be considered to be "cotexts" with the operative report in that their referent is an aspect of the surgical event. Many of these texts are created by professionals other than the surgeon. Prior to the operation, the patient is evaluated by an anesthesiologist, and this evaluation is noted on the progress notes. The patient signs a consent form prior to the operation stating that he or she has been informed of the nature of the operation by the surgeon, and that he or she consents to the operation. The hospital where this research was conducted is unique in that it has a preoperative holding area. This area was created since there is a high percentage of high risk patients receiving surgery so that they can be closely monitored prior to surgery. this monitoring is recorded. (See Appendix D.)

Unlike operative reports, which are created after the operation, some documents are created during the operation itself. The anesthesia report (Appendix E) is completed by an anesthesiologist (physician with a specialty in anesthesia) or nurse anesthetist. Nursing notes (Appendix G) are also recorded during an operation, and include such items as the patient's condition, the types of drains, implants, and packs used, the sponge count, and the names of all personnel present in the operation.

Following the operation, the patient's condition is monitored and recorded in the postanesthesia recovery room (Appendix G). The pathology report is relevant to the operation also, and is the pathologist's macroscopic and microscopic evaluation of tissue removed during surgery. A handwritten operative note is written on the progress notes by a member of the surgical team immediately following surgery as well. (See the following section for further detail on this report.)

Purposes of the Medical Record

The medical record serves a variety of functions, both during the patient's stay in the hospital and following discharge. In this section, I discuss the overall purposes of medical records; in the following section, I discuss the purposes of operative reports more specifically.

While the patient is in the hospital, the medical record serves as a means of communication and planning among the professionals who care for the patient (Joint Commission on Accreditation of Hospitals 1987). Physicians write orders for medication and other treatment on the medical record; nurses and other professionals record that they have carried out the treatment on the medical record. Other professionals, such as dieticians, chaplains, occupational and physical therapists, and social workers, meet with the patient to discuss concerns relevant to their area of expertise. All these plans and discussions are recorded on the patient's medical record.

Another purpose of the medical record is to provide "documentary evidence of the course of the patient's medical evaluation, treatment, and change in condition" (Joint Commission on Accreditation 1987:95). In practice, this frequently means that "the medical record is not the *record* of medical practice, it *is* the medical practice" (Weed 1971; emphasis added). It has been argued (Frankel in press) that, in actual clinical practice, the patient and the medical record are used in such a way that, for all practical purposes, the two are equivalent. For example, in research which examined videotapes of doctor/patient interaction, the physician was observed to consult the medical record before questioning the patient (Frankel 1981). A more anecdotal example of the importance placed on the medical record is that a patient recently told me that she requested a copy of her medical record in order to understand what had happened to her during the course of her last hospitalization. She requested her record so that, in case she were readmitted to a teaching hospital, she could give a more accurate commentary on her disease when the many interns and residents who would see her would ask "What's wrong with you?" Or, as in the Baby Doe case (*New York Times,* 1984), federal regulations now require that federal investigator, examining infants at risk on the basis of hotline tips, must go first to the hospital infant-care committee rather than to the nursery to examine the patient. This seven-member committee, consisting of a practicing physician, hospital administrator, nurse, attorney, a representative of a disability group, a citizen, and a member of the medical staff, would most likely use the medical record as a source of information in order to make decisions regarding the infant's care and to verify observations regarding the infant. Here, since infants cannot speak for themselves, the medical record and the committee serves as their intermediaries. In other words, the patient's medical record is the intervening document between one practicioner and another and this document is, no doubt, often accorded more credibility than the actual patient.

Following the patient's hospitalization, the medical record is not merely filed away, but is used for a variety of purposes. I discuss here, first, two new developments that have occurred within the past decade and which have resulted in a new and more important status of the medical record within the hospital bureaucracy: the use of the medical record to determine Medicare prospective payment and the role of the medical record in quality assurance.

Recent Medicare legislation has created a closer link between medical records and the financial operations of the hospital. For Medicare patients, the medical record is now the source document which determines the extent to which Medicare will reimburse the hospital for that patient's treatment (Currie 1985, Serluco and Johnson 1983). The patient's final diagnosis, in effect, determines the amount that Medicare will pay to the hospital. This final diagnosis is categorized with one of 468 Diagnosis Related Groups (DRGs), and Medicare reimburses the hospital a flat rate for each DRG. As a result, DRGs are claimed to provide financial incentives for hospitals to offer services more efficiently. Other factors such as surgery performed, comorbidities and/or complications, and the patient's age, sex, and discharge status influence the DRG assignment. Of prime importance, then, for financial reimbursement is the principal diagnosis, which must be given in terminology compatibile with the ICD-9-CM coding system (Cofer 1985) as well as the documentation of any secondary diagnoses and other related factors named above, all of which are encoded from the medical record.

Quality assurance (QA) is also a relatively recent innovation which expands the role of the medical record. In answer to the many malpractice cases of the past decade, QA is the hospitals' attempt to impose quality controls on health care (Skillicorn 1981). JCAH standards require that hospitals initiate comprehensive ongoing reviews of health care within each department the hospital's jurisdiction (Warner 1985, Mehnert 1985, Joint Commission on Accreditation 1987). Each clinical and administrative department within the hospital is therefore responsible for identifying problems within that department's area, defining the suspected causes of the problems, proposing solutions, and monitoring the status of the problems. The new QA standards differ from previous clinical review activities. Now, each department within a hospital is involved in defining quality of care for that particular department, and in setting up methods to analyze that quality. In the past, this was considered to be primarily a function of only the clinical departments.

The medical record has historically been the source document for clinical review activities. The expanded role of QA places the medical record in an even more critical role, not only after the patient is discharged, but also during the time that the patient is in the hospital. JCAH is encouraging hospitals to look at sources other than the medical record to evaluate the quality of care, however. (Joint Commission on Accreditation of Hospitals 1981).

Whether or not the medical record is adequate to demonstrate the quality of care given has been a topic of debate in the medical literature. Donabedian (1966) states that recording on the medical record is a legitimate dimension of medical practice in and of itself. Not only that, recording is the medium of evaluation by which other dimensions of medical practice are evaluated. Payne (1979) suggested that the medical record is the only source of information concerning physician performance. Examining quality of care as evidenced through the medical records in ambulatory care settings, Payne (1979), in contrast to Fessel and Van Brunt (1972), reaffirmed the conclusions of an earlier study (Lyons and Payne 1974), that stated, "Studies of different populations, with different levels of analysis at different times, in different geographic areas, with different measures, using different research designs in both hospital and office settings converge to the finding that (1) good recording is related to good practice, and (2) the relationship is not perfect, but it is statistically significant" (Payne 1979:628). Nonetheless, in practice, the JCAH (1981:12) is somewhat skeptical about the quality of information on the medical record:

> Although many review and evaluation requirements indicate that the medical record should be used, the QA standard broadens this interpretation. Many other data sources and approaches can be used to identify problems more quickly and more effectively. In fact, the medical record may not contain the information needed to determine the cause and scope of a problem—lack of documentation often hinders assessment of a topic in traditional audit studies, and improvements of documentation often becomes the focus of study because health care professionals assume that appropriate care was provided but not documented.

Traditionally, the medical record has also been the source document for other postdischarge activities besides DRGs and quality assurance. The medical record is used for medicolegal purposes, to protect the interests of the patient, the hospital, and the practitioner (Joint Commission on Accreditation of Hospitals 1987). (There is an extensive bibliography of the medicolegal use of the medical record, and I discuss the medicolegal implications of operative reports more extensively in Chapter 5.) The medical record is also used in epidemiological and retrospective research (cf. Kurland and Molgaard 1981, Cherkin, Phillips, and Gillanders 1984, Horwitz and Yu 1984). As a result, the medical record is a crucial source document for a number of clinical and administrative purposes.

Creation of Operative Reports

Operative reports, like other reports on the medical record, are subject to standards of the JCAH and have a more or less conventionalized format that is used in hospitals across the United States. As such, it is an example of a *genre* (Swales 1986:4), or a "recognized communicative event with a shared public purpose . . . and within variable degrees of freedom, a structured and standardized communicative event with constraints on allowable contributions in terms of their positioning, form, and intent." In this section, I give an overview of standards relating to operative reports, and I describe in general terms the content of operative reports (for a more complete and in-depth description of a report, see Chapter 3). I then present the hospital events that occur when an operative report is produced.

According to JCAH (1987:100) standards,

Operative reports are dictated or written in the medical record immediately after surgery and contain a description of the findings, the technical procedures used, the specimens removed, the postoperative diagnosis, and the name of the primary surgeon and any assistants . . . The completed operative report is authenticated by the surgeon and filed in the medical record as soon as possible after surgery . . . When there is a transcription and/or filing delay, a comprehensive operative progress note is entered in the medical record immediately after surgery to provide pertinent information for use by any practicioner who is required to attend the patient.

I discuss each of these requirements separately, and how they unfold in practice in one large midwestern teaching hospital affiliated with a medical school. This commentary is based on a year's fieldwork, including observations of three operations and in-depth interviews with seven surgical residents, as well as discussions with an assistant professor of surgery and a medical records administrator.

In practice, immediately following an operation, the patient is taken to the Postanesthesia Recovery Room. There, the resident, surgeon, or medical student writes a written note on the progress noes describing the operation that was performed (see Appendix A). This note is usually a listing of the abstracted "facts" about the operation, such as the names of the surgeons, assistants, the pre- and postoperative diagnosis, the procedure performed, fluids replaced, and whether any drains were left in. Handwritten postoperative notes by a resident or medical student are authenticated by the attending surgeon. In complex cases (Appendix B), this handwritten note may contain sketches of various facets of the operation. The report in Appendix B was of gastric carcinoma. One sketch shows where the tumor was located, and the other shows where the stomach was excised and the intestine attached to the remainder of the stomach.

As stated earlier in the chapter, the resident or surgeon dictates the operative report in the dictating area in the surgeons' lounge. Residents attempt to dictate the operative report immediately following surgery, but their schedules may prevent them from doing so. One resident estimated that this occurs 50% of the time. It seems common that residents learn from experience not to let their uncompleted operative reports accumulate. It is difficult to remember what happened from one operation to another, and the residents that I interviewed made it a practice not to leave the hospital for the day unless their dictation was complete. The hospital administration imposes sanctions on physicians who do not complete their assigned dictated reports, or who have not signed certain reports. Periodically, the medical records department notifies the chiefs of various departments of the residents who have reports to dictate and/or sign. The chiefs of the department then use their influence to require residents to dictate the reports. In rare occasions, the residents' paychecks are withheld until the reports are completed, or the residents cannot officially complete the training program until all reports are done.

The operative report itself is a typewritten summary of the procedures and findings of an operation (see Appendix C for an example). It is standard practice in all hospitals to list and space certain information at the beginning of the report. The date of surgery, the pre- and postoperative diagnoses, the names of surgeons and assistants, and the type of anesthesia are indicated here.

The textual section of an operative report typically consists of one or two sections. The *operative technique*, which is a narrative text of the operation, is always included. The report in Appendix C is not unusual, in that the operative technique section is physically one long paragraph; it is not divided into paragraphs. At this hospital, surgeons and residents may also include an *indications* section. This section gives the clinical circumstances that led to the operation. Some residents and surgeons choose to include an indications section for all operations; others include it for medicolegal reasons only if the patient is to undergo a risky procedure. In a case such as this, the surgeon would include an indications section, in order to state that the patient was informed of the risks involved in the operation. In some hospitals, although not in the one where this fieldwork was done, surgeons may divide the operative report into *operative findings* and *operative technique*. Here, rather than having the findings interspersed within the narrative account of the procedure that was followed, the findings are given first in a separate section.

As with other reports on the medical record, the report must be authenticated by the attending surgeon in the case that it was dictated by a resident.

Purposes of Operative Reports: a Subclassification Based on Audience Needs

Operative reports, as part of the patient's medical record, are subject to the purposes described in the preceding section: for quality assurance evaluation, and for DRG, medicolegal, and research purposes. However, an operative report may be more or less important for future clinical or administrative purposes, depending upon several factors. In order to discuss these factors, I would first like to speak generally of the role of the operative report within the surgical event.

In order to place the operative report within the context of the event of surgery, let us first consider, in general, the role of talk within the context of an event (Levison 1979:368):

On the one hand we have activities constituted entirely by talk (a telephone conversation, a lecture for example), on the other activities where talk is non-occurring or if it does occur is incidental (a game of football for instance). Somewhere in between we have the placing of bets, or a Bingo session, or a visit to the grocers. And there are sometimes rather special relations between what is said and what is done, as in a Sports Commentary, a slide show, a cookery demonstration, a conjuror's show, and the like.

I would like to extend the notion of the role of talk within an activity to the role that reporting plays within the activities that occur during the course of a hospitalization. While the relationship between reporting and event within the hospital bureaucracy is extremely complex (see Raffel 1979), it appears that this relationship can be roughly categorized in three ways. The following discussion focuses primarily on this relationship for purposes of medical communication rather than for purposes of bureaucratic accountability. (See, for example, Garfinkel 1967.) In hospital medical records, the relationship between reporting and the accompanying medical event is as follows:

(1) Reporting of communication between professionals constitutes the primary purpose of the event. Some activities that occur during the course of a patient's hospitalization are done primarily to communicate information to the physician responsible for the patient's care. The report constitutes the end result of that activity. A prime example of such an activity would be reporting on pathology. The pathologist examines tissue excised during an operation and, as a consultant, communicates the findings and opinions to the surgeon (Wagner 1984). While this communication may first be oral, as during the course of an operation where carcinoma is suspected (see Chapter 2 for further discussion and an example), the final definitive report is written to be filed on the patient's medical record. Without the communication of the pathologist's findings, the examination of tissue would be a meaningless activity; the patient's interests would not be served without this communication.

Other examples of types of activities where the reporting is the main focus and purpose of the event include reporting on an autopsy, reporting on x-rays, nuclear medicine examination, and other types of clinical laboratory reports.

(2) Another type of relationship between event and reporting is a post hoc relationship. In other words, some type of care is given to the patient, and, subsequent to that care, the event of the care is reported on. In this type of activity, communication between specialists is not necessarily the focus of the activity. Reporting on an operation would be an example of a post hoc relationship between event and report. For some operations, the primary objective is to perform the procedure, such as taking out the appendix, rather than to examine a body part for further diagnostic purposes. The

relationship between event and report is more complex than this, of course, and I discuss these complexities in more detail in the following section. Nonetheless, it is fair to say in certain cases that, if an operation is performed, the patient would improve whether or not the surgeon communicated the results of the operation to anyone.

(3) The third type of relationship between event and reporting is a mixed relationship. Here, performing the care is the purpose of the activity, but, because of the nature of medical decision making and of accountability of medical personnel to the attending physician, reporting on the activity plays an important role. Consider, for example, nursing notes. Nurses provide various types of care for the patient which directly affects the patient's clinical course. Since much of the care is based on orders given by the physician, nursing notes indicate compliance with those orders. Care is reported to physicians who are vertical on the organizational hierarchy. Nursing notes also communicate horizontally from nurses on one shift to another. Nurses, in order to assess the condition of the patient, may rely on the observations of nurses from the previous shift.

Regarding the relationship between the surgical event and recording on that event, I stated previously that, in some cases, the patient would improve whether or not the surgeon communicated the results of the operation to anyone or not. This is a simplified observation of what is, in fact, a much more complex phenomenon. I would now like to amplify the communicative role of the operative report, and in particular, discuss the interest that potential audiences would have for any one report. For any particular operative report, a number of factors determines who these potential audiences are. The principal factors are the patient's diagnosis and where the operation occurs in the course of the patient's illness. The audience for these reports depends, then, in part on the role of the surgical event in the illness of the patient. I present three types of potential audiences, plus contingencies that may change the interest that various groups may have in the operative report. This audience typology is based, in part, on observations made by a surgical resident. He also supplied examples of the diagnoses.

(1) Memorandum for file. I term the first group "memorandum for file"[2] because there is, in effect, very little audience interest for these types of cases. Here, the operative report is like a memorandum to be filed away for bureaucratic and legal purposes. Let us return to the notion of an operation as an event. We can think of the operation as an event that terminates or abates the illness. Following some postoperative recovery, the

---

[2]This observation from a discussion with Dwight Stevenson. This section on audience is also influenced by Mathes and Stevenson (1976).

patient returns to health, and there is no further need to consult the operative report. Such cases would include amputations, appendectomies, and incision and drainage of abscesses. These procedures, in most cases, are rarely called into question over whether the procedure is appropriate in light of the diagnosis, and they terminate the condition that brought the patient to the operating room. (See Chapter 5 for further implications of memorandum for file cases.)

(2) Adversary audience.   In effect, these are cases where, because of the operation, the case might result in legal action. In these cases, the surgical event, rather than terminating a particular illness, creates a new chain of circumstances which may result in life changes or a new illness for the patient. The two examples presented here are somewhat different in terms of the adversarial nature of the audience, but, since this is a rough typology, they are categorized together.

Surgery of the hand, while it may be performed to correct problems caused by an accident, poses future disability problems to the patient. Operative reports of hand surgery are frequently requested in order to evaluate the extent of disability in workmen's compensation cases. Although the legal interest in these reports is not necessarily adversarial *against* the surgeon or the hospital, the document is required to be precise in order that the extent of disability may be determined.

Cases in which intraoperative complications occur are also cases which could be requested by an adversarial audience. Here, the operation is not one of a chain of events (accident–operation–litigation), as with hand surgery, but is the instigating factor that causes an adverse effect on a patient. The common example that comes to mind here is the malpractice case in which an instrument or a sponge is left behind during surgery.

(3) Medical audience.   In these cases, the patient has a troublesome problem, such as cancer, which will require future medical attention. Needless to say, categories (2) and (3) are not mutually exclusive. An operative report of interest to an adversary audience is, of course, of interest first to a medical audience. It is not unusual that family members, frustrated by the lack of progress of a cancer patient, may institute a suit against the surgeon. (Surgical resident, personal communication, May 30, 1984). In cancer cases, then, the surgical event may be only one step in an ultimately terminal process. Therefore, for future medical caregivers, it is extremely important to pinpoint the stage of the disease and to describe precisely the observations of the area being examined. Frequently, the type of surgery performed for cancer is complex, and it is important to describe which parts are taken out, which parts are left intact, and which parts are attached to others. (Cf. Appendix B for a sketch of this in a cancer case. The sketches are described verbally in the dictated operative report.)

Moreover, these reports are used in determining chemotherapy protocols. These drug treatments may be designed on the basis of the surgeons' observations of the affected area.

(4) Contingencies.   In the event of a *contingency*, particularly a postoperative complication, any type of operative report may be examined by a medical audience, in particular, and in some cases, by an adversarial audience. For example, if the patient has a fever following an operation, or severe and unexplained pain, the operative report would be examined by physicians to determine what had happened during surgery and whether additional treatment were warranted. If a postoperative complication is severe enough, and if the patient ultimately sues, then an adversarial audience would be interested in the report as well.

Background of This Study

Although some research has examined the process of reporting certain texts on the medical record (cf. Garfinkel 1967, Cicourel 1974, 1975, Frankel 1981, Treichler, Frankel, Kramerae, Zoppi, and Beckman 1984, van Naerssen 1985), or has been concerned with the computerized encoding of clinical narratives (see Johnson, Tsao, Bross, and Shedd 1979, Sager et al. 1982), very little research has examined the process of reporting on operations. Research which has examined operative reports has been concerned with standardizing the information in these reports so that they may be encoded for computer storage (Shapiro 1967, Bross, Shapiro, and Anderson 1972),[3] or has been concerned with examining the discourse motivation for certain sentence types in the reports (Pettinari 1983, 1985).

My previous research, like much research in discourse analysis as well, has addressed the text as a completed, or received, entity. Recently, however, some research which examines texts, particularly in the philosophy of science, has begun to provide detailed access to the construction of scientific papers (cf. Knorr and Knorr 1978, Latour and Woolgar 1979, Garfinkel, Lynch, and Livingston 1981, Knorr-Cetina 1981, Gilbert and Mulkay 1984). The present study is indebted to this research (as well as to that research which examines the process of medical reporting mentioned above) in that it, too, studies the relationship between the text and the reality from which the text originates. The focus of the present study is different, however, in that it is concerned to a greater extent with linguistic and sociolinguistic factors in the "reality" from which the text comes. It is

---

[3]Interestingly, the computer research did have a linguistic basis, in that the "automatic coder of report narratives" (Acorn) relied on kernel sentences (Harris 1968) as the point of origin to develop a standard notation for information storage.

also more concerned with an in-depth thick description (Geertz 1973) of the discourse structure of the texts. (Knorr and Knorr 1978, Latour and Woolgar 1979, and Gilbert and Mulkay 1984 do deal with rhetorical structure of texts, however.) Moreover, the goal of creating a scientific research paper differs greatly from the goal of creating an operative report, of course. The "reality" of the work of science is focused towards the goal of the creation of the scientific research paper. Through the research paper, the scientist contributes knowledge to a particular field. Careers are made on the basis of the quantity and quality of research papers that the scientist produces. Operative reports, on the other hand, are part of the ongoing work of a surgeon, and, as previously discussed, may not necessarily be the prime focus of the surgeon's activity, nor are they specifically examined for quantity or quality.

Operative reports are an example of an instance of language as part of an activity or "language game" (Wittgenstein 1958) common in our society. This activity is the creation of textual records of crucial activities taking place either within or under the auspices of bureaucratic institutions. Police reports, personnel reports, and reports of x-rays, surgery and autopsies are all written narrative documentation of a professional's observation and description of a person, event, or procedure. While such records may be crucial to the persons reported on, to the professional involved, and to the functioning of the organization itself, very little research has examined the actual process of recording these observations and descriptions.

Furthermore, the choice of information selected to be recorded, and its grammatical form, have rarely been examined or described from a linguistic point of view. Even though language plays the central role in this type of recording, little is known about how language in records is shaped by the organizational context or the records' purposes. Moreover, while part of professional competence is the creation of such records, the language game of creating these textual records is rarely formally taught, nor has the acquisition of such genres been studied.

This Study

This study adopts the point of view of examining the learner's role in the language game of creating the textual records. The general purpose of the study is twofold: (a) to examine the role of the learner in the process of text-building which produces the final written legal document of the operative report, and (b) to examine the process of change of reporting styles over time by surgical residents as they progress through their training. These objectives are achieved via a series of case studies. As with studies which use the case study method, the results from the small sample are yet to be generalizable. I accept the view of Bernhardt (1981:7) that:

> Such an approach attempts to preserve the situational integrity of each instance of language activity, rather than obliterating the organic nature of individual texts through statistical descriptions of the "average" text based on a large sample.

The first objective of this study derives from recent work in functional discourse analysis and what has also been termed "modern philology" (Becker 1980). These studies are concerned with examining ways in which the context shapes and is shaped by the particular text itself. One of the basic aims of such studies is to expose and interpret "distant" texts as a language act in light of the context in which they were created, so that the texts may be understandable and readable to the modern American reader. In these studies, "distant" is generally considered to be culturally and linguistically far from the analyst. This study recognizes that medical texts produced in a bureaucratic institution such as a hospital can be considered as "distant" in the sense that they not only have a specialized lexis and structure, but that there is a particular interaction of constraints which result in that text.

Foucault (1973) notes the precedence of language in all stages of a medical investigation: from the noting of symptoms and the questioning of the patient, to the description of the state of physiological functions, to history taking, to noting the progress of the disease, and finally to the prescription to the patient. What happens in the case of illness which requires treatment in a hospital is that all of these stages of medical investigation are textualized onto the patient's medical record through the workings of the bureaucratic organization of the hospital. The influence of the hospital bureaucratic organization may be lesser or greater depending upon the type of text. For example, some texts, such as patient histories (Cicourel 1974, 1975, Frankel 1981, Treichler et al. 1984), may be simply handwritten during or following consultation with the patient. Other texts, such as operative reports, pass through several contexts and stages in the creation of the final written legal document.

Chapter 2, then, examines the process of the text-building of operative reports. Chapter 2 takes into account two of the contexts and stages which combine to create the final written legal document. Other than deconstructing the final, completed entity, as is common in most discourse analysis studies, this study examines the first two points of the successive contexts which produce the final written legal document:

1. the operation itself
2. the transcription of the record of an operation

2. final revision (if necessary) and signature of the typewritten text by the physician
3. the final signed official legal document

In Chapter 2, then, the relationship between the talk that occurs in an operation and the resident's dictation of the operation is examined. In this chapter, a dramaturgical metaphor (Goffman 1959) is used to categorize the talk that occurs during an operation which had two procedures: examination and removal of a gastric tumor (gastrotomy) and removal of the gallbladder (cholecystectomy). The operation and the dictation of the operation by the resident was audiotaped, and observational notes were compiled by the researcher. The talk in the operation is categorized into language acts which are clearly "backstage" in that the talk is for the benefit of the team; these language acts are not recorded on the operative report.

"Frontstage" language acts, such as the talk concerned with diagnosing the tumor, is recorded on the operative report. In Chapter 2, I demonstrate, however, that, as the operation proceeds in time, in the talk, the diagnostic label becomes more and more specific. Furthermore, the construction of the diagnostic label of the tumor is, to some extent, a sociolinguistic process. During the course of the operation, the diagnostic label is more or less hedged (Prince, Frader, and Bosk 1972), depending upon the role relationships of the members of the surgical team. An examination of the temporal sequence of the operative report reveals that this increasing specificity of diagnosis is not captured in the operative report examined in this study, nor is the sociolinguistic construction of the diagnosis.

Other instances of talk can be considered a mixture of frontstage and backstage activity for reporting purposes. Traces of these activities appear on the operative report. In particular, planning and medical decision making occurs in the talk of the operation; in Chapter 2, the relationship between these elements and the reporting on the operation is examined.

The second goal of the study is to examine the process of change of reporting styles over time by surgical residents as they progress through their training. In this section of the study, I attempt to answer the question: how do operative reports produced by surgical residents change as the resident gains experience in reporting on the surgery?

In order to understand these texts, in this section of the study, we first need to understand the plot of texts, or the "set of constraints on the selecting and ordering of episodes or motifs" (Becker 1980:226). In other words, we need to know which features of the operation are generally selected to be included in these reports and which are not, and then what the order of those features are.

Thus, prior to attempting to answer the above question, in *Chapter 3*, an in-depth study of one report is done. Chapter 3 describes a cholecystectomy performed for the first time by a first year resident. The resident's dictation of the operation is both audiotaped and observed by the researcher, and the final written text is collected. A methodology for determining episodes is set up, whereby the author of one text, that is, the resident who dictated that report, aids in determining what constitutes an episode. In the in-depth analysis, the methodology for analysis takes into account the transformation of texts mentioned above, and is also informed by the resident's segmentation of the text into episodes.

Following the segmentation into episodes, variables such as grammatical cues and prosodic features, which are claimed in the discourse analysis literature (see van Dijk 1982, Chafe 1980) to correspond to episode boundaries, are investigated. In this chapter, rather than considering the spoken and written versions of the text as two separate entities, in the in-depth analysis, one form of representation informs the other. In this analysis, the relationship between the spoken and written texts is examined as a process and is also informed by the segmentation of the text into episodes by the resident.

The purpose of the analysis in Chapter 3 is to provide a unit of analysis with which to study the longitudinal data in *Chapter 4*. In Chapter 4, the macrolevel of episode is chosen as a point of entry into the analysis of cholecystectomy operative reports dictated by five fifth year residents of one residency training program. Data collected and analyzed include the first and final cholecystectomy reports dictated by each resident at one residency training site. The fifth year residents were also interviewed to determine criteria (Payne 1979) of information considered important to include. In Chapter 4, the change in content of the operative reports, and the ways in which the content are expressed linguistically is examined. In some sense, the beginning reports can be considered as "writer-based prose" (Flower 1981) in that the apparent concerns of the beginning residents come first, and the final reports can be considered to be "reader based prose" in that the readers of these reports' needs are taken more into account. In beginning operative reports, writer-based prose includes information which might be most salient to a beginning resident, such as the instruments used in the procedure and various transitional devices which move the narrative of the procedure along. Reader-based prose, in the final reports, contains more emphasis on the findings of the operation, as well as "chunking" of the narrative of the procedure.

In *Chapter 5*, I return to the way in which the context is influenced by the text. In this chapter, medicolegal considerations of the study are summarized and discussed, and practical applications of the findings are suggested.

CHAPTER 2

PROCESS OF TEXT-BUILDING OF OPERATIVE REPORTS

This chapter examines the process of text-building from which results the final written document of an operative report. In the construction of the final written legal document of an operative report, several contexts result in the final written text. These contexts include:

1. the operation itself
2. the dictation of a record of the operation
3. the transcription of the record of the operation
4. final revision and signature of the typewritten text by the attending surgeon

In this chapter, the relationship between contexts (1), the operation itself, and the dictation of a record of the operation (2), is examined.

Previous Research

A few studies have examined the relationship between talk in a medical context and the recording of information from the spoken discourse on to the medical record. An early study of information on the medical record (Garfinkel 1967), had as its impetus the problems that researchers had in finding information from psychiatric clinic records for sociological studies. Although the study did not deal explicitly with the talk from which a medical record derives, routine demographic data were not necessarily recorded on these records or the data were difficult to find. Garfinkel observed that the lack of data resulted from "normal natural troubles" because personnel in the clinic have well established procedures in reporting their activities. These established ways of reporting are, in part, devised against the possibility that the therapeutic relationship "may have to be portrayed as having been in accord with expectations of sanctionable performances by clinicians and patients" (p. 199). A reading of clinic records, when viewed with this purpose in mind, rather than revealing an order of interaction, presupposes that the reader understands such an order prior to their reading.

Cicourel, in a pair of studies (1974, 1975), examined the relationship between the questioning that occurs in medical interviews and the summary of this information onto the written summaries for medical record purposes. The first study was concerned with information processing problems associated with decisions made during medical history interviewing. Cicourel noted that the written summary of the interview did not reveal the reasoning that the physician used in asking questions, and in deciding that appropriate answers had been given. In fact, according to Cicourel, when a specialist asks questions and receives answers in the medical context, this reasoning is rarely revealed in the medical history report. A problem, therefore, may exist because a physician from another specialty may not be able to reconstruct reasoning based on the medical history.

In this earlier paper, Cicourel hints that the physician follows a schema or script (Schank and Abelson 1977) in asking the questions, but does not consider explicitly the possibility of the existence of such a script for the written medical summary. In the interview, the physician is hypothesized to follow an implicit outline based on his or her experience with patients having the same condition.

In the later paper, Cicourel (1975) deals more specifically with the possibility of the existence of a script or schema that guides the construction of the medical summary. In examining how these summaries could be analyzed according to a story grammar (Rumelhart 1975), Cicourel concedes that story grammars provide a formal structure that can represent a story, but these grammars do not indicate how a writer decides what is relevant or irrelevant to include in these stories. In the case of an interview of a nonnative speaker of English in which there were a number of difficulties in establishing facts, "a coherent summary was obtained despite inadequate, misleading, fragmentary and incomplete information elicited in the interview" (p. 57). In other words, the summaries that were examined gave the "appearance of a convincing and factually correct account of the patient's problems" (p. 58), despite the interactional problems in the interview. In effect, medical summaries are compared to a "folk practice" where stories are told in fairly standardized ways, even though the original experience may not have occurred in quite this way. Cicourel notes some bureaucratic consequences of this. Medical summaries can lead to "decisions, bureaucratic consequences, and aggregate reporting of information" (p. 58) that seldom take into account the circumstances under which the data are collected, or the medical reasoning behind the information recorded on the summary.

More recently, Treichler et al. (1984), in examining power relationships in medical encounters, consider medical record recording that occurs during the course of a medical encounter as one dimension of the physician's exercise of power. Since recording on the medical record while interviewing provides multiple foci of attention, it robs attention from face-to-face interaction. During the course of a doctor/patient interview, using video-tape, this study maps each incidence of writing to the ongoing talk between physician and patient. Treichler et al. observe that "what is said and what is recorded do not necessarily stand in a one to one relationship" (p. 71). Furthermore, the psychosocial complaint that brought the patient to the physician is not recorded on the summary, thereby it lacks "official" status.

Thus, recent research into the relationship between spoken medical discourse and written medical reports has primarily examined reporting that ensues from doctor/patient interaction. The reporting examined in this chapter differs from these studies in some respects. First, the operative report does not derive from spoken questions from physicians to patients about their medical condition and history. Rather, the talk is between professionals. The anesthetized patient is not part of the interaction. Since the talk in the operation is between a number of professionals, albeit at varying levels of a known chain of command, the medical reasoning that takes place is more likely to be revealed in the talk.

The spoken discourse in an operation is somewhat reminiscent of "shop talk" (Lynch 1979) that occurs among scientists in a research lab. Shop talk, according to Lynch, is the talk that occurs as part of the ongoing laboratory activity. It is not "idle chatter" that might be part of a coffee break, or to relieve boredom, but is inseparable from the work scene, an integral part of the activity. The details of the work activity are presupposed as features of the work that can be seen. The talk itself cannot be isolated from the work scene; in the absence of the work, the talk is meaningless, as there are a number of implicit references to the work being done. Lynch found that shop talk is "ethnographically strange" in that a number of terms, generally understandable by the lay person, are used in special ways. Shop talk appears to be like "ordinary conversation" in a number of ways, in that jokes are part of the talk and there are no special phonological features to distinguish it, yet the participant-observer, Lynch himself, could not participate in the shop talk. Another feature of shop talk is that gaps of silence occur. Topics continue across the gaps, and a silence does not necessarily indicate an absence of activity.

Features of the talk that I observed in the operation appeared quite similar to shop talk, with the additional sociolinguistic feature of participants at different levels on the chain of command. Therefore, a number of linguistic features that indicate status differences, such as hedging, mitigation, and topic initiation by the participant with the highest status, were observed.

The operative reports themselves (see Appendix H for the resident's operative summary examined in this chapter), while summaries, of course, differ from summaries of doctor/patient interaction as well. They are not summaries of questions and answers in a medical interview with the patient, nor is the patient as explicit a referent in the account. Rather, operative reports are summaries of procedures performed on the patient. As such, perhaps operative reports share some similarities with the *methods sections* of scientific papers. Methods sections are "highly conventionalized accounts of what the authors did" (Gilbert and Mulkay 1984:52). In the methods sections of scientific papers, the procedures that were followed are described, but in an idealized, but not necessarily chronological, fashion. Operative reports describe procedures that were followed, as well as observations about the patient's anatomy. (See Chapter 4 for a more complete discussion.)

The Operation

The operation that was observed was an exploratory laparotomy (surgery to explore and examine the abdomen) which was performed to examine and remove a mass in the patient's stomach. Prior to the surgery, the surgeons explained to me that the patient might need a gastrectomy (removal of the stomach), since it was suspected that the patient's abdominal mass might be malignant. During the operation, the stomach mass was found to be benign, and, as a result, the stomach was not removed. A gastrostomy, that is, an incision into the stomach, was made to remove the stomach mass instead. There was another mass in the patient's abdomen, a porcelain gallbladder. Removal of this mass necessitated an additional procedure, a cholecystectomy, to remove the gallbladder.

The surgical team consisted of the chief surgeon, a fifth year resident who assisted at the surgery, a medical student, and two nurses—a scrub nurse and a circulating nurse. A scrub nurse has sterilized hands and is responsible for handing instruments to the surgeons. A circulating nurse does not have sterilized hands and, as the name implies, moves throughout the operating room. Two anesthesiology personnel were also present: a nurse anesthetist who was present at the entire operation, and an anesthesiologist (physician with certification in anesthesiology), who came into the operating room for part of the operation. There were two observers at the operation: a nurse in training and myself. During the course of the operation, the attending surgeon's partner passed through the operating room and talked with the surgeons. Of the active participants in the operation, the chief surgeon, resident, anesthesiologist, and surgeon's partner were male; the medical student, nurses, and anesthetist were female.

Immediately following the operation, the resident went into the physician's lounge in the operating suite to dictate the operative report. There is a separate room in the lounge with telephones to use to dictate the reports. The dictation goes to a centralized dictation area, where medical transcriptionists transcribe the taped dictation.

Data Collection

The operation and the resident's dictation were audiorecorded with a battery powered hand-held Panasonic RQ-356A tape recorder using a Sound Grabber pressure zone microphone, model 12-SG. The sound quality of the tapes of the operation was poor because of numerous high pitched sounds in the operating room: anesthesia equipment, suction and hemostat equipment, the amplitude of the patient's breathing, and paging sounds, along with many other unidentifiable sounds. Because the surgeons wear masks, and because their heads are within inches of each other when they talk during the operation, their speech is often inaudible to both the tape recording and also to others in the operating room. Although I was only a few feet away from the surgeons myself, on some occasions I could not hear what they were saying, much less capture the sound on a microphone. (There were no problems in hearing the resident's dictation, however.)

In transcribing the tapes for analysis, I was able to alter the quality of the tapes somewhat by use of a graphic equalizer to remove or lessen the very high pitched and low pitched sounds. Nevertheless, there are fairly large segments of talk which I was simply unable to either hear or transcribe. Of those audible sections of tape, there are sections where the physicians lowered the amplitude of their speech, and, since I was unable to hear some parts of the audible sections well enough to transcribe them, there were some gaps in the transcription.

Other reasons for difficulty in transcribing the tapes resulted from the physical nature of the operating room itself; the walls, ceiling, and floor are tile, and sound echoes a great deal in such a room. A number of conversations occur simultaneously during an operation as well. Nurses converse together; the anesthetist and anesthesiologist discuss the patient's condition at the same time that the surgeons talk. In fact, what I found interesting in transcribing the tapes was that there was almost constant talk during the operation.

Because of the difficulties in hearing the tape, the linguistic transcription itself is not as precise as in that designed by Jefferson (Schenkein 1978). Overlaps and pauses are not noted at all times. In my transcription, parentheses indicate uncertainty about the working of a section; . . . indicate inaudible sections of talk.

Besides the constant talk during the operation, I also found the topics of discussion audible enough to be heard interesting in and of themselves. Discussion of the abdominal masses was quite audible, as were a number of language acts such as asking for instruments, joking, instructing, planning, and asking anesthesiology for readings of the patient's condition.

Relationship Between Talk in the Operation and Information on the Operative Report

One way of thinking about the relationship between the kinds of language acts that occur during an operation and the reporting of information about the operation is to use a dramaturgical metaphor (Goffman 1959).[1] In this metaphor, the person in everyday social and work situations presents himself or herself to others and attempts to control the impressions that others form of him or her. In attempting to influence others' perceptions, the person employs certain techniques in order to maintain the performance. In case studies of particular social establishments, Goffman believes that the actions of teams of workers is the basic point of reference from which to study the management of impressions that an audience to a professional performance has. In such social situations, there is "backstage" activity that only the team has access to, and "frontstage" activity that the audience knows about. In the operation discussed here, some of the talk that occurs is clearly backstage; humorous comments and conversation are interactions between members of the surgical team which have little relevance to the needs of the potential readers of an operative report on the medical record.

Other instances of talk can be considered to be mixtures of backstage and frontstage activity for reporting purposes, and traces of these activities appear on the operative report. As an example, members of the surgical team may formulate a plan to perform certain parts of the operation, but the formulation of that plan does not appear on the report of the operation. Only the end result of performing of the act is reported on. In other words,

---

[1] I would like to thank Rich Frankel for reminding me of the relevance of Goffman's work here.

here the planning is backstage activity, and the end result of the plan is frontstage. Similarly, what might be frontstage activities or the professional focus of one group's activities, such as monitoring the patient's condition by anesthesia professionals, is considered backstage for reporting purposes by the surgeons, and so such information is not repoirted on in the operative report, but is found in other sections of the patient's medical record.

Other instances of talk are frontstage in the sense that the topic that is talked about in the operation is considered important for the potential readers of the report, and is reported in the operative report. However, because of the strong narrative "driving" script (Schank and Abelson 1977) of the reporting of the operation, the order in which the events actually unfold in the operation may not be captured in the narrative reporting on the events in the operation. As Cicourel (1975) notes, the folk practice of telling the story supercedes the real order of events. In this case, when the resident reports on events in the operation he orders them in the way that they are typically sequenced in the operative report, whether or not they actually occur in that order.

In the following sections, I discuss these three types of language acts and the ways in which they are revealed in the operative report. I proceed from those language acts not found on the operative report, to those in which traces are found on the operative report, to those topics which are talked about in the operation and are reported on in the operative report as well.

Language Acts not on the Medical Record

Not surprisingly, those language acts which indicate interpersonal relationships among the operating room team, such as humorous remarks and conversation, are not recorded on the patient's operative report. There is no organizational purpose for devoting precious time and resources to recording them. Although medicine is thought to be a very serious business, as with science (Gilbert and Mulkay 1984), it does, in fact, contain a strong undercurrent of humor. Those language acts which go to make up humor appear to be very important for a sense of solidarity among the members of the operative team in the operation. Humor may also be used as a relief of tension, given the potential seriousness of the situation.

Humor appeared to be one means to achieve a sense of solidarity among the members of the surgical team, and it also appeared to be used for exercising social control by the surgeon and the resident. In observing this operation, I had a sense that the operating room nurses enjoyed working for this particular surgeon. Before the operation began (it was on Monday morning), the nurses said that they felt lucky to be scrubbing for two operations for this particular surgeon; it would help the week begin well. As an indication of the backstage nature of the performance I was about to observe, when one nurse was told that I would be audiotaping the operation, she asked me, "Does this mean that we can't tell jokes?"

In fact, in this operation, very few jokes were "told." The type of humor in the ongoing talk of the operation consisted of spontaneous witty remarks, almost all of which were initiated by the surgeon. The topic of the majority of these comments were members of the surgical team, in particular, ironic remarks about the resident's skill as a surgeon. No humorous remarks were made about the patient. The following is an example of a remark made to me by the surgeon about the resident (in this section, I call the attending surgeon "the surgeon" and the resident surgeon "the resident." When grouping them together, I refer to them as "the surgeons"):

> *Dr.*: He's one of those guys who train in the Babinski School of uh
> Operative Summary Dictation where uh brevity is uh
> *Res*: next to godliness
> *Dr.*: ((laugh))
> *Res*: ((laugh))
> *Dr.* c'n I have another (cord) please? I told you about that portal caval
> shunt of Babinski, didn't I?
> *Res*: yeah. That was a page, wasn't it?
> *Dr.*: less than a page. six lines long . . .

In fact, examining the place of humor in the talk of the operation indicates the strong social control that the surgeon exerted in the context of the operation. In this case, as in others, the surgeon opened the floor for more humorous comments by beginning to talk about the resident. It is important to remember that, while *all* instances of talk that are given in this chapter take place as part of the ongoing activity of surgery (for example,note the side sequence of a request that the surgeon made: "c'n I have another (cord) please?"), humorous remarks appear to be made during the more routine parts of the surgery. No joking took place during more clearly stressful parts of the operation such as removing the tumor.

As with humor among scientists (Gilbert and Mulkay 1984), the humor resulted from two incongruous ways of viewing something. The chief incongruity (and the source of humor for other comments in the operation) was the juxtaposition of two divergent interpretive frameworks: one being the surgeon's obvious high opinion of the resident (as seen in other parts of the operation and in remarks to me on other occasions), and the other in statements hinting at his lack of ability. In the above example, humor results from naming a School of Operative Dictation (no such thing exists, of course) after a former resident known for having done a short operative report. ("That portal caval shunt of Babinski" refers to a report of an operation of a portal caval shunt that was dictated by a former resident named Babinski.) There may be a teaching message to the humor here as well. This surgeon is letting the resident know that a report whose length is inappropriate to the complexity of the procedure does not go unnoticed.

The resident was often the "straight man" in the joking. The resident apparently did not resent the joking; in fact, he told me on another occasion that he felt "friendly and chummy" with this surgeon.

Participants in the operation are clearly organized hierarchically, both in terms of the formal organizational structure and in terms of responsibilities in the operation. In every operation done in a teaching hospital, a licensed surgeon is present and has the principal responsibility for the performance of the procedure. Residents assist in the operation. Depending upon the attending surgeon's judgment of the resident's skill, he or she may delegate parts of the procedure to the resident. To examine this aspect of teamwork that occurs in an operation would be better captured with videotape than audiotape, as the passing back and forth of responsibility appears to be nonverbal as well as verbal. The way in which the surgeon, resident, and medical student each perform aspects of the procedure and pass responsibility back and forth occurs in a fascinating rhythm.

Because of the necessity of precision and delineation of responsibilities, the extent of each participant's responsibilities are clearly stated and understood. This hierarchical structure appears to be reflected in the fact that, as previously mentioned, the surgeon initiated the great majority of informal talk and humorous comments during the operation. In other words, the surgeon sets the tone for where moments of levity are allowed. Other instances of witty remarks were initiated by members of the operating room team at the same hierarchical level as the surgeon is: the anesthesiologist and another surgeon who passed through the operating room during the course of the operation. The resident, lower on the organizational hierarchy, did not initiate informal conversation or joking, but on one occasion he did cut off a remark initiated by the nurse anesthetist, which indicated incongruity. This remark could have led to more joking, but didn't:

Res:	(to medical student, about the gastric tumor) Yeah, it's been there. It's probably a while now. (With a benign) they'll outgrow their blood supply and (slough on) and bleed and that's what you . . . just feel it (right there) feel it. Isn't that sompin? Feels free in there, doesn't feel like it's going through the wall
NAnes:	(is that like) when you swallow your gum always . . . and your mother said . . .
Res:	You don't have her NG on suction, do you?
NAnes:	

No, I don't.

Res: Good. And is it taped to her nose?

NAnes: yes it is

Rather than answer the question from the anesthetist about the gastric tumor being like gum that was swallowed as a child, the resident "denies the dialogic frame" (Goffman 1981) initiated by the anesthetist by returning the dialogue to the part of the activity of performing the operation. In fact, he challenges instead the nurse anesthetist's performance of a responsibility (Labov and Fanshel 1977). In so doing, he asks the anesthetist two "obvious" questions; he can see for himself the answer to one of them ("and is it taped to the nose?")

We can only speculate, of course, the reason for not following through with the topic initiated by the anesthetist. One reason, I feel, is that the topic gets close to personal commentary on the patient. References to the patient as a person, such as her life, background, personal habits or appearance, were very rare during the talk that I observed in this operation. In fact, the only personal reference to the patient occurred towards the end of the operation, where the resident explained, in answer to the medical student's question, why the patient had waited a long time to have the surgery done. Other references to the patient during the course of the surgery related more to her ongoing condition, such as blood pressure and blood loss. References were also made about the patient's good condition during the course of the operation in light of her age.

Other reasons for cutting off the attempt at humor may relate to the hierarchical organization of the operating room team; a fifth year resident is in a more superior position than a nurse anesthetist. The resident was male and the nurse was female, and this may have been a factor in denying the frame offered by the nurse. This may be one more example of the tendency in this culture not to reward women for being funny (Kramerae 1981).

Another instance of joking can be seen in the verbal sparring that occurred between the anesthesiologist and the surgeon, as in:

Dr.:   (to me) Pretty boring idn't it?

CP: ((laugh))

Anes: not the surgery, just the surgeons.

The only instance of conversation of a nonmedical nature that took place between the physicians that was audible enough to be transcribed was an interchange between the surgeon and the resident. Again, the surgeon initiated the talk:

Dr.: so you lost some money on Saturday, huh?
Res: yeahhhh lost a little bit. There was a pool n I lost seven bucks in it. I had three horses for it, yknow. n one of em didn't come up n win. Even had the horse my dad thought was one
Dr.: which was
Res: Silent King or . . . sompin I can't I can't remember. I like Gate Dancer. I'm lucky I had him for the (Della Rusia) one of em was his third straight Derby win
Dr.: He might come up whether he's . . . or not. This was his first win, wasn't it?
Res: I'm not sure, maybe his first Derby win
Dr.: He's a veteran . . .
Res: is he?
Dr.: oh yeah ((at this point, the resident's responses are inaudible))

The previously discussed language acts, joking and conversation, take place between and among the participants in the operation, and there is no organizational purpose to record them on the report of the operation.

Another language act which does not appear on the report of the operation is any teaching or instruction that takes place during the operation. Since the hospital in which the operation took place is a teaching hospital, one of its organizational functions is to provide instruction to a variety of students: medical students, nursing students, medical technologists, and others. Instruction is provided both formally, in classes and seminars, and informally, as in the apprentice-like training that occurs in the real job situation. In this operation, since there were medical personnel of various levels of expertise in attendance, from an assistant professor of surgery to a fifth year resident to a medical student, instruction occurred during the course of the operation. Early on in the operation, the resident explained about the tumor to the medical student:

Res: (Benign tumor — on the top of the stomach) . . . put your hand down in the stomach and feel it. In the stomach and feel that (hole) in there.
(horn)
Medical student: hmm
Res: Isn't that sompin?
MS: (It sure is different)
Res: Yeah it's been there. It's probably a while now. (With a benign) they'll outgrow their blood supply and (slough on) and bleed and that's what you . . . just feel it (right there). Feel it. Isn't that sompin? Feels free in there, doesn't feel like it's going through the wall.

Here, the resident identifies and points out the tumor to the medical student, states its location, estimates the length of time that the tumor has been there, and gives some instruction about the nature of a benign tumor. This type of instruction is more explicit than the coaching and encouragement that the surgeon gives the resident during the part of the procedure where the tumor is taken out:

Res: now I'm gonna cut this up n put it up here too
Dr.:   uh
Res: d'y say like that? or cut it like sompin here? in that manner, hun?
Dr.:   (you could go down there)
Res: Yeah that (leaves) a blood loss
Dr.:   mm hm
Res: but (I could) slow. What d'ya think (names himself)?
Dr.   cautery!
Res: right here in the (ad) joints stay close to it!
Dr.:   close to it
Res: right
Dr.:   good
Res: mm hm
           ((cautery sound))
Dr.:   mm hm. (Resection) here
Res: (touch) here
           ((cautery sound))
Dr.:   (you cd get closer here)
Res: yeah I know it's . . .
           ((Cautery Sound))
           ((paging sound))
Res: mm hm (almost at home)
Dr.:   . . . stay up close. Not *too* close (Girtz) . . . see up there? There's tumor there.
Res: That's . . .
Dr.:   Probably. Probably a little piece of it there. I don't see don't see (tumor there now)
Res: mm hm

Here, the resident states what he is going to do and then asks for advice on which approach to take. The surgeon gives an alternative, and, since the referent for *that* in the utterance by the resident ("yeah that (leaves) a blood loss) is unclear, it is not certain whether the alternative suggested by the surgeon is chosen or not. The request by the surgeon ("cautery!") to the scrub nurse is indicative of a request for action of a different kind, a part of the ongoing sequence of multiple levels of talk to the participants in the surgery. As has been noted in linguistic studies of pediatrician/ mother/child interaction (Tannen and Wallat 1982), the surgeon here is balancing a number of demands at one time, many of which are language related. In this case, he is advising and coaching the resident, requesting instruments, and performing the actions of the surgery. Following this, a series of utterances then almost echo each other (as where the resident says "mm hm" and the surgeon says "mm hm. Resection here." The resident then says "(touch) here.") Later the surgeon offers advice (you could get closer here) and continues the coaching as to how close to get.

The final two language acts not recorded on the operative report that I will discuss are requesting assistance to make adjustments to the surgeons' clothing and repositioning the patient.

At one point in the operation, the resident requested help in readjusting his mask and glasses:

Res:	Listen you gotta fix this up a little bit. This's driving me crazy. My glasses fall down my face y'know? All ya gotta do is loosen this up n pinch it down around my nose
Male voice (anesthesiologist?):	tape it a little bit. tape'd be better
Res:	won't do it. Can't put tape on (it) t's my fault. Should not put tape on (the case) all ya gotta do it . . .

All of the above sections refer to interactions between members of the surgical team. One language act which refers to the patient and is not recorded on the operative report is requesting the repositioning of the patient towards the end of the operation:

Res: c'n we put her in a little reverse Trendelenberg please? Feet (forward?)

The written report on surgery does not reveal the above interactions, such as humorous comments, conversation, and teaching among the members of the surgical team, no doubt because such language acts are not of interest to the potential readers of the report. In a sense, humor and conversation can be considered to be purely interactional "backstage" activity between the participants. Although they take place during the operation, they bear no real relationship to the ongoing activity of performing the particular operation. Instructing, on the other hand, especially the kind of coaching discussed in the previous section, is collaboration that is more relevant to the activity of the operation. In reporting on such activity, however, there would be a necessity to personalize the participants in the operation, which is rarely done in these reports. While there may be some relevance to delineate the specific role that each participant plays in a particular operation for malpractice defense purposes, to my knowledge this is not commonly done. This may be because, in any event, the attending surgeon is ultimately responsible for the conduct of the operation.

Information That is Partially on the Operative Report

In this section, I discuss other types of collaboration among the operative team of a more specifically medical nature. This collaboration includes making decisions about various facets of the operation and planning approaches to take. Such activities are indicative of medical decision making. As with summaries of doctor/patient interaction (Cicourel 1974, 1975), medical reasoning is generally not revealed explicitly in the summary of the event, however. The operative report, like the summary of a doctor/patient interview, is a "legal document that indexes the application of medical knowledge, but does not permit a reconstruction of the contingencies" (Cicourel 1974:65) of the event that produced the summary. In the case under investigation here, the collaborative nature of the activities of decision making and planning does not appear on the report of the operation, although the end result of the collaboration and decision making may be recorded on the report. In other words, the decision making is considered to be "backstage" activity, whereas the result of the decision making is "frontstage" for reporting purposes.

In this operation, approaches to various parts of the procedure were discussed and planned. Advice was given about which approaches were to be taken. At one point in the operation, a decision had to be made about where the tumor was anchored in the stomach, and a plan was formulated for taking the tumor out:

Dr.:   Feel that lesion there
Res: yeah (it's a little sac) Hold that while it's (the trunk) you move it you move it right over it. The whole *front* wall's free from it. The only question is where's the tag
Dr.:   where's it anchored
Res: it's *anchored* on the *poster*ior I think up *high*. It's up probably up at the middle of the junction. You can get - c'mon just feel, I mean it's so moveable you can open that thing and it'll shell right outta there
Dr.   OK, let's, we're uh we've got this greater curvature. We'll be able to uh pass her out
Res: Hemostat. We got right angles in there? Waiting there?
Nurse: mm hm

The resident's dictation of this part of the operation does not reflect the collaboration involved in finding the location of the anchoring of the tumor and in planning how to take out the tumor. Rather, a unitary point of view without mention of participants is reflected in the report:

The lesser sac was first approached, which is opened and all of the greater curve was taken down between hemostats, divided and tied with 3-0 silk. The short gastric is left intact. Having accomplished this, enough of the stomach was freed up, so that two stay sutures of 3-0 vicryl could be placed in the anterior wall.

In the operating room talk in the preceding segment, two topics of conversation appear: deciding the location of the point of anchoring of the tumor, and planning how to take out the tumor. Both of these reflections of medical decision making are the result of collaborative activity between the resident and the surgeon.

By contrast, the report reflects a decontextualized unitary point of view, and it is difficult to determine what stretch of talk produced it. The report, like methods sections of scientific papers, appears to be "a catalogue of sequential manipulations stripped of context and rationale" (Knorr-Cetina 1981). The report gives no indication of the number of language acts that result in deciding the location of the point of anchoring of the tumor. In fact, in the report, although the location of the tumor is stated, no specific mention is made of the point where the tumor was anchored in the stomach.

To return to examine other features of the talk in more detail, we can also see both hedging and planning. Hedging is not revealed in the operative report and neither is the particular plan observed here. In the hedging talk, the resident observes that the whole front wall is free of tumor. The resident and physician overlap in their questioning of "Where's the tag" "Where's it anchored?" The resident observes that the tumor is "anchored on the posterior, I think, up high. It's up probably up at the middle of the junction." At this point in the talk, the resident hedges. In Prince et al.'s (1982) terms, the speaker uses a *plausibility shield* to indicate that the speaker is asserting a belief acquired by plausible reasoning, as opposed to deductive logic. In other words, in contrast to deductive logic, plausibility reasoning indicates the likeliness of a proposition. In this case, the resident may also be hedging because he is speaking to a superior. In any event, the operative report does not reveal the above decisions or hedging involved in the medical decision making.

The planning that occurs in this segment of talk includes determining how to get out the tumor. One way of looking at planning discourse (Linde and Goguen 1978) has been to consider that plans are structured in a tree structure. For example, Linde and Goguen schematize one simple realization of a plan as follows.

GOAL/PLAN

FUTURE STATE   HOW TO ACHIEVE IT

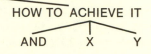

In the case of this segment of talk in the operation, the plan for removing the tumor could thus be schematized as follows. Note that, here, "open that thing" and "shell right out" may be examples of "ethnographically strange" phrases (Lynch 1979) that no doubt have precise technical referents.

GOAL/PLAN

FUTURE STATE   HOW TO ACHIEVE IT
Taking out tumor

                                          AND   X   Y
          AND   "open that thing" "shell right out"

This particular plan is not recorded in the report of the operation. In fact in this segment of report, the grammar of the text suggests that another plan could be inferred:

GOAL/PLAN

FUTURE STATE   HOW TO ACHIEVE IT
placement of 2 stays sutures   free up stomach

In a sense, as Cicourel (1974) states, the plan in the operative report may be considered to be more indicative of the application of medical knowledge (in that a finer level of detail of the procedure is indicated in placing of sutures results from freeing up the stomach) than the actual construction of medical knowledge (in order to take out the tumor, something must be opened and the tumor shelled out).

Another aspect of medical decision making that is not completely revealed in the medical record is the process of ruling out other possible diagnoses. Although, in many cases, the diagnosis is determined prior to the surgery, in this particular case, it was uncertain whether the tumor was malignant prior to the operation. As a result, the final diagnosis of a benign tumor took place during the course of the operation, and the diagnosis of a malignant tumor had to be ruled out. The most definitive way to do this, of course, is by sending frozen section of tumor to the pathology lab for examination and the pathologist calls the results to the operating room. Also, however, the surgeons make other examinations and observations during the course of the operation to determine the likelihood of malignancy. These examinations include determining whether there is studding of the liver with tumor and whether there are tumor implants in the abdominal wall. These factors are generally ruled out during the part of the operation in which the abdomen is explored (surgical residents, personal communication, May 15, 1984). In the following segment, the abdominal cavity has been opened and the resident is pointing out about the tumor to the surgeon.

Res: Dr. _____ , I bet this is benign. A little ball sittin in the stomach
Dr.:   Really?
Res: I wonder whaddya think about opening this. ⌈ Maybe
Dr.:   ⌊ Maybe
        can we wait
Res: (maybe) lettin me feel it? (Y'know) Feel like ya open n just shell
        thethink out. Whaddya think? You see what I mean, this (messy)
        stomach feels real free. It's ts ball sittin in there.
Dr.:   n'nothin looks like its anything else outside?
Res: no
Dr.:   (rs is)
Res: (this is) well she's had operations before y'know? I'm gonna start lookin
        at the rest of it
Dr.:   liver's OK?
Res: so far . . . my Bovie
.   ((Deleted section))
Res: The left lobe of the liver is completely clean and see this is all, this is all
        adhesions here (so let's get rid of em)
        (inaudible because of background noise)
Dr.   (you're doing such a good job)
Res: Dr_____ Dr _____ here
Dr.:   (inaudible)
Dr.:   (Here's your bold stroke here)
Res: yeah it's — it's take it down (in a triangular way) here. Some adhesions
        really get stuck (rest and ya hafta) (yknow)
        (20.0)
Res: interesting ain't it?
Dr.   (unbelievable try a split finger cath hold in it)
Res: idnt it? n'it didn't feel like it's down in all the walls

The resident's dictation of this part of the operation, the exploration of the abdomen, states:

The abdominal cavity is entered. There are numerous adhesions which must be taken down sharply on either side of the abdomen for final freedom and adequate exploration. The left lobe and right lobe of the liver are free of any masses or tumor. The aorta is of normal size and no aneurysmal dilatation of the vessels. Colon and intestinal structures seem to be without masses. The stomach can be easily palpated and has a very freely moveable baseball size mass within its upper portion. It does not penetrate through the wall of the stomach. There are no celiac nodes.

In the report, the sequence does not precisely follow the sequence of events in the surgery. To return to the talk, it appears that the order of events in the operation (e.g., the examination of "anything outside" and examination of the liver) are the events that would lead to a differential diagnosis of a benign tumor. Further collaboration between the resident and surgeon are shown in the surgeon's encouraging the resident as the adhesions are taken down, and further plans are made for how to remove the adhesions.

The report does not make transparent this order of events that indicates the medical decision making process. The report begins with removal of the adhesions, and it appears, from reading the report, that the adhesions were taken down *prior to* the exploration of the other items in the abdomen, such as the liver and the stomach. In fact, the transcript of the talk reveals that the surgeons examined the left lobe of the liver and noted the mass in the stomach before taking down the adhesions. The order of events in the report is not structured in the same way as the events in the surgery which rule out the other possible diagnosis of malignancy.

Instruments

Instruments, sutures, and drains are other elements of surgery that the person dictating the operative report may or may not choose to record on the operative report. (See Chapter 4 for further discussion of how first year residents include more of such information in the operative report.) One common stereotype of talk in the operation is the surgeon interjecting "scissors!" "sponge!" This type of request does, in fact, occur. However, there are other, more mitigated, means by which surgical implements are requested in this operation. In other words, a variety of linguistic means are utilized in order to mitigate the request, or to avoid giving offense (Labov and Fanshel 1977). Types of mitigating devices in this operation, for example, include the surgeon's or resident's ability to obtain an item (e.g., "cn I have a fresh pack please?") and whether the nurse has the item being requested (e.g., "y'got the Vicryl?") Generally, in this operation, only instruments are requested by name (e.g., "scissors!"), and sutures, packs and saline are requested in more mitigated fashion (see Table 2.1).

What is interesting about the relationship between the requests for surgical implements,[2] and the inclusion of these implements in the report of the operation, is that those items that have been requested with a mitigated request, i.e., sutures, packs, and saline, are more likely to be recorded on the report of the operation, than are instruments, which are requested with

---

[2]Saline is also included here under implements or equipment for purposes of description, since it was an item requested of the nurses.

Table 2.1. Surgical Implements Requested During the Operation

Form of request	Requested by surgeon	Requested by resident	More than one request
Metz (Metzenbaum scissors)		X	2
	X		
Kocher		X	
scissors		X	3
hemostat		X	3
	X		4
uhhh pickups		X	
cautery	X		
alright suction	X		
scissors	X		
suture scissors	X		
(Bell) Metz		X	
suction		X	
Clamps			
we got right angles in there? waiting there?		X	
right angle		X	4
Sponges			
sponge	X		
sponge here?	X		
what's the smallest sponge you got up there?		X	
gotta sponges?		X	
Packs			
How about a Bell pack?	X		
cn I have a pack please?		X	
hey got a fresh moist pack there?		X	
Suture material			
y'got the Vicryl? 2–0? 3–0?		X	
cn I have some of that 3–0 vicryl?		X	
cn I have some vicryl?		X	
. . . . . . 3–0 vicryl		X	
(3–0 with that)		X	
. . . . . . if those silks are ready		X	
Other			
tie	X	X	
cn I have another (cord) please?	X		
cn I have a skinny little Dever?		X	
you got pickups?		X	
Can we have some (more) normal saline for irrigation?		X	
I'd like a change in gloves. Dr. _____ would too before we (close this now)		X	
cn I have some irrigation?	X		

a direct imperative. In the report, there are 12 mentions of sutures, two of packs and three of saline, whereas there is only one mention of instruments.

The following are the audible requests for surgical equipment. They are categorized into type of item requested, and the person requesting the item (S = surgeon; R = resident) is also given. Note that instruments are requested only by naming them directly, whereas packs and suture material are requested with a mitigated request.

The last section that I discuss is information which is both found in the talk in the operating room and is actually dictated onto the operative report. In this section, I trace the development of the talk about the gastric tumor and relate that talk to the description of the tumor in the operative report. I point out here that, even for those topics which are considered important to be included in the operative report, i.e., tumors, the talk does not necessarily stand in a one-to-one relationship to the reporting on those topics. By this I mean that, as with the medical decision making previously discussed, the order of events in the operating room talk does not necessarily match the order of events in the operative report. The description of the tumor is an emergent phenomenon, a complex social event not totally captured in the reporting on the operation.

A somewhat similar phenomenon was observed in real-time videotape examination of doctor/patient interaction by Treichler et al. (1984). They noted that the physician's entry on the medical record has "no tie whatsoever with the ongoing discourse" (p. 71). In that study, what the physician was writing, e.g., the date, was not the same information that the patient was giving at that particular moment, e.g., the list of ailments.

The reporting on an operation is clearly not an online phenomenon, as is the note taking that occurs during a doctor/patient interaction. However, the synoptic distanced point of view that the fifth year resident utilizes in reporting does not reflect the ongoing discovery process that occurs during the operation that determines the nature of the tumor. I suggest that the narrative script (Schank and Abelson 1977) that the resident employs to describe the operation influences the way in which the operation is reported on, but it does not fully capture the actual unfolding of events in the operation. Note that some of the data discussed in this section is the same as that presented in the previous section on information which is partially on the medical record. In that section, my purpose was to point out sections of talk that illustrate medical reasoning that may or may not appear on the operative report. In the present section, I am interested in an overview of the discovery process of the tumor and the reporting of that discovery on the operative report. In developing this section, rather than discussing the operating room talk first, as I have done in previous sections, I present the operative report first. This is done in order to clarify the order of events that the resident uses in reporting on the tumor.

The Gastric Mass

In the operative report, the description of the stomach mass comes *at the end of* the section of the report which describes the exploration of the abdomen. In most operative reports, the section that describes the exploration of the abdomen is generally found immediately after the section which describes making the incision. (See Chapter 3 for a more complete description of episodes that go to make up an operative report. It may also be, although I have not investigated this issue, that the organ of interest is mentioned *last* in the exploration of the abdomen section of the operative report.)

> once through skin
> subcutaneous tissues
> linea alba and peritoneum
> the abdominal cavity is entered
> and there are numerous adhesions which must be taken down sharply on either side of the abdomen for final freedom and adequate exploration
> this found left lobe and right lobe of the liver are free of any masses or tumor
> the aorta is of normal size
> and no aneurysmal dilatation of the vessels
> colon and intestinal structures seem to be without masses
> the stomach can be easily palpated and has *a very freely movable baseball size mass within its upper portionit does not penetrate through the wall of the stomach*

Upon reading this report, one might suspect that the stomach mass was found after the other organs were examined, as the description of the mass comes at the end of the section describing the exploration. As is typical with fifth year residents (see Chapter 4 for further discussion), this resident uses a complex noun clause to describe an anatomical entity encountered during the course of the operation: *"a very freely movable baseball size mass."* In other words, when the anatomical feature is encountered in the report, it is described with a number of adjectives and nouns preceding it. The location of the mass is described in a prepositional phrase "within its upper portion," and, in the successive clause, a significant negative finding is stated: "it does not penetrate through the wall of the stomach."

The order of events in the surgery does not parallel that in the operative report, however. The examination of the gastric tumor occurred shortly *after* the abdomen had been opened, and *before* the other parts of the abdominal cavity were examined. In the dialogue, we see the resident explaining to the medical student about the tumor:

Res: (Benign tumor . . . on top of the stomach) . . . put your hand

	down here in the stomach and feel it. In the stomach and feel that (hole) in there (horn)
Med stud:	hmmm
Res:	Isn't that sompin?
Med stud:	(It sure is different)
Res:	Yeah it's been there. It's probably a while now. (with a benign) they'll outgrow their blood supply and (slough on) and bleed and that's what you . . . just feel it (right there) Feel it. Isn't that sompin? Feels free in there, doesn't feel like it's going through the wall

At this point, the resident identifies the tumor as being benign and located on top of the stomach. He does not feel at this point that it is going through the wall. He hedges in stating that "it's probably a while now." Shortly after this, the resident talks about the tumor to the surgeon:

Res:	Dr I bet this is benign. A little ball in the stomach
Dr.:	Really?
Res:	I wonder whaddya think about opening this? ⌈ maybe
Dr.:	⌊ (maybe
	we can wait)
Res:	(maybe) lettin me feel it? (y'know) Feel like ya open n just shell the thing out. whaddya think? You see what I mean, this (messy) stomach feels real free. It's ts—ball sittin in there
Dr.:	n nothin looks like it's anything else ⌈ outside?
Res:	⌊ no
Dr.	(rs is)
Res:	(this is) well she's had operations before y'know? I'm gonna start lookin at the rest of it
Dr.:	liver's OK?
Res:	so far . . . my Bovie

When the resident introduces the tumor to the surgeon, he hedges in stating "I bet" it's benign. As previously discussed, the surgeon asks if anything else is outside and the resident states that it is not. At this point, the exploration of other organs in the abdomen is begun.

Let us return now to examine more precisely how the tumor is described in the operative report. In the operative report, four factors describe the mass:

1. mobility: a very freely movable
2. size: baseball sized
3. location: within its upper portion

4. significant negative findings: it does not penetrate through the wall of the stomach

These factors have been talked about in the operation up until this point in the following ways:

1. mobility: R to MS: "feels free in there"
2. size: R to S: "a little ball in the stomach"
3. location: R to MS: "on the top of the stomach"
4. significant negative finding: R to MS: "doesn't feel like it's going through the wall" This is confirmed with S to R: "n'nothin looks like it's anything else outside?" R: "no."

In the ongoing unfolding of the discovery process about the tumor, one factor has appeared in the talk that has not appeared in the report at this point: the fact that the resident believes the tumor is benign.

Let us return now to the description of the abdominal mass in the operative report. (See Appendix H for the sequence of the entire operative report.) Following the previously mentioned section in which the abdomen was explored (lines 40–59), the resident continues to describe the process by which the mass in the stomach is excised (60–91). In the report, following that description, the cholecystectomy procedure is then described (92–115). After the section that describes the closing of the abdominal wall and the sponge and needle counts (116–129), the gastric mass is again referred to. Here, the report from pathology on the mass (130–131) is given. This report from Pathology is almost at the end of the operative report. It states:

the frozen section on the mass in the stomach came back as a benign probable leiomyoma.

Again reading this section in the sequence of the report, it would appear that the frozen section came back from Pathology towards the end of the operation. In fact, the report from Pathology came back at the end of the part of the procedure where the mass in the stomach was taken out, and prior to taking out the gallbladder. The resident announces the termination of the section of the operation dealing with the stomach, and states that the gallbladder will now be operated on:

Res: Close the stomach n then we got a gallbladder gallbladder to take out

In terms of the sequence of events, after this announcement, a beeper sounds and the pathologist reports to the surgeon over a loudspeaker:

Path:	Room 2?
F voice:	Hello?
Path:	yes
Path:	d'doctor _____ calling on the frozen
Dr.:	yeah
Path:	((names his full name)) a single cell neoplasm (totally) benign. Looks like either a (neurolemoma) or a leiomyoma
Dr.:	you think it's benign though, right?
Path:	yeah
Dr.:	That's what it looks like, fine
Path:	can you uh, listen did you get most of it?
Dr.:	yeah
Path:	OK so you didn't
Dr.:	we didn't leave any behind. Started . . . n we could see (one stalk of it) n we cut into it, but we went below that then
Path:	OK, fine. Will there be more tissue coming then?
Dr.	no
Path:	OK Thank you
Dr.:	*Thank you*

From the talk in this section, we can learn two things that are different from the report:

(1) The order of events is different in the operation than in the report.

(s) In the unfolding of the diagnosis of the abdominal mass, the verbal report from pathology was that the mass was "either a (neurolenoma) or a leiomyoma." In the operative report, the resident stated that the mass was a "probable leiomyoma." There appears to be some difference between the amount of hedging in the operative report and the spoken report on the frozen section. In the operative report, the mass is called a "probable" leiomyoma, but, in the call by Pathology, the mass is said to "looks like either a (neurolemoma) or a leiomyoma."

The dictated operative report implicitly gives the responsibility for naming the mass as a leiomyoma to the Pathology Department; nowhere else in the report is the mass so explicitly named. However, in the talk in the operation, the surgeons do suggest that the mass is a leiomyoma. Before the tumor was taken out, another surgeon walked through the operating room and the following conversation occurred:

Res:	hi
Other dr:	well? is it a . . .
Dr.:	it's probably just a benign uh
Res:	leiomyoma
Dr.	leiomyoma

At this point, the surgeon hedges and both the resident and surgeon overlap in naming the tumor. But, during the part of the operation where the tumor is being taken out, the following conversation ensues which is not hedged:

Female voice: what is it?
Surgeon: It's a leiomyoma of the stomach.

Finally, to return again to the operative report, in the heading section of the operative report where the names of the surgeons, the pre- and postop diagnosis, type of anesthesia, and patient identification data are listed (lines 1–14 on Appendix I), the preoperative diagnosis is called *gastric mass*, as is the postoperative diagnosis. The gastric mass is not diagnosed more specifically than this by the resident for either the preoperative or postoperative diagnosis.

To summarize this section, then, I would like to present two tables which describe the discovery process in describing the tumor. The first (see Table 2.2) is an abstract of the operative report. This table gives the points of the discovery process in the same order as they are in the patient's operative report, and includes information that is only found in the operative report.

This is information on the gastric tumor abstracted from the operative report. Note that the information becomes nonspecific from the beginning to the end of the report as the information is formatted on the actual report. In other words, the operative report starts with the preoperative diagnosis as "gastric mass," and the final discussion of the mass in the report is a "benign probable leiomyoma." There is a problem here, however. The problem is that the postoperative diagnosis "gastric mass" is not as specific as the commentary on the tumor at the end of the report. The reason for this may be that the postoperative diagnosis is located on the report out of real time sequence on the physical format of the operative report. Because

Table 2.2.   Information about the Gastric Mass on the Operative Report in Temporal Order

Name	Agent or Person Naming the Mass
Preop diagnosis	
gastric mass	not stated
Observations Prior to surgery	
no palpable mass	physical exam
a large mass in the stomach	CT scan
Observations During surgery	
stomach can be easily palpated and has a very freely moveable baseball size mass within its upper portion	(surgeon implied)
benigh probable leiomyoma	frozen section
Postop diagnosis	
gastric mass	not stated

of this, perhaps, the final determination of the name of the mass is "gastric mass," whereas much more specific labeling of the mass happens in the operation. Note also that there is not any hedging in the operative report, and that it is difficult to determine who is responsible for naming the tumor.

Table 2.3 illustrates how the tumor was described in the talk in the operating room. In the social construction of the labelling of the gastric mass during real time, there is considerably more hedging, dependent, perhaps, upon the relative standing of speaker and hearer in the operating room hierarchy. Another reason for hedging may be the extent of the certainty that the surgeon or resident feels at that particular moment. Furthermore, as with the operative report, the labelling becomes more specific, but we are able to trace the persons who have named the tumor. Table 2.3 traces that sequence. At the end of both of these charts should come one more report (which I did not obtain) which occurs in the labelling of the tumor, the final written pathology report of the tumor. The pathology report gives the definitive description of the tumor.

Conclusion

In conclusion, this chapter examined the relationship between a number of language acts which occurred during the course of an exploratory laparotomy and the reporting of the operation. The language acts were classified into three types: (a) those which were not recorded on the

Table 2.3. Description of the Gastric Mass in Real Time

Name	Agent
Preop diagnosis	
gastric mass	not stated*
Observations Prior to Surgery	
no palpaable mass	physical exam*
a large mass in the stomach	CT scan*
Observations During surgery	
(benign tumor . . . . on top of the stomach)	Resident to med stud.
Feels free in there. Doesn't feel like it's going through the wall	Resident to med stud.
I bet this is benign. A little ball in the stomach	Resident to surgeon
It's probably just a benign leiomyoma.	Resident and surgeon to other surgeon
It's a leiomyoma of the stomach	Surgeon to unidentified female
A single cell neoplasm (totally) benign. Looks like either a (neurolemoma) or a leiomyoma	Pathologist to surgeon
It's a big benign leiomyoma	Surgeon to other surgeon
Observations Following surgery	
?	Pathology report

* = found on operative report, not available from audiotape or talk

operative report, (b) those in which traces were recorded on the operative report, and (c) those topics which are talked about in the operation and reported on in the operation.

Talk, such as humorous comments, conversation, and instruction, examined in (a), while not considered important to report for institutional purposes, does reveal significant "backstage" (Goffman 1959) activity indicative of status on the organizational hierarchy. The surgeon is in control, initiating topics and humorous comments during more routine parts of the operation.

In (b), medical reasoning is more transparent in the kind of "shop talk" (Lynch 1979) that occurs among professionals in the operation than in previously studied doctor/patient interactions (Cicourel 1974, 1975, Tannen and Wallat 1982, Treichler et al. 1984). This chapter examined some instances of medical reasoning and planning not revealed in the operative report. The decontextualized format of the operative report appears to mitigate against their inclusion. It could be that, if this were a case where medical reasoning might come into question for one reason or another, then that medical reasoning might be made more explicit. It would seem, however, for the information of other specialists, as Cicourel (1975) notes, that the medical reasoning that occurs in surgery might be of interest as well.

Finally, the talk that occurred in the operation which centered around the naming and labelling of the tumor revealed that such labelling is a sociolinguistic process, complete with hedging and other manifestations of status relationships. Such sociolinguistic processes are not captured in the operative report. In this particular case, the postoperative diagnosis recorded was no more specific than was the preoperative diagnosis, despite the ongoing specificity of the labels that applied to the tumor. The actual physical layout of the operative report may be one reason for this.

CHAPTER 3

THE NARRATIVE STRUCTURE OF OPERATIVE REPORTS

Introduction

The previous chapter examined the relationship between talk in an operation and the reporting on that operation. The concern in this chapter is to determine the narrative structure of one type of operative report: cholecystectomies (an operation to remove the gallbladder). The goal of the analysis here is to determine the plot or the "set of constraints on the selecting and ordering of episodes or motifs" (Becker 1980:226) for this particular type of text. A unit of analysis, an episode, is thus determined. This unit will then aid in analyzing the contrast in reporting styles of beginning residents and of fifth year residents in Chapter 4.

As in Chapter 2, data are gathered from the several contexts which produce the final text, and these contexts are taken into account in the analysis:

1. the operation itself
2. the dictation of a record of the operation
3. final revision (if necessary) and signature of the typewritten text by the physician
4. the final signed official document

In this chapter, my particular focus is on (2), the oral dictation of the operation, and (3), the transcribed version of the report. The analysis in this chapter recognizes that the dictated and written versions of the reporting contain different types of linguistic cues which may enter into the analysis of the text. In addition, an interview was conducted with the resident who performed the operation, to determine how he would segment that event as he looks at the dictation. The interview aids in determining whether a parallel exists between the way in which the events are spoken about and the way in which the events are written about.

This chapter includes both the methodology and the in-depth analysis of one operative report of a routine cholecystectomy. After discussing the data, I briefly point out that there are two macrolevels of structure of this text: (a) the formatting of certain information on the page of the report, and (b) the episodic structure of the narrative summary of the operation. I review the discourse analysis literature of received texts which examines the division of texts into an intermediate level between the text and the sentence, or what I have chosen to term *episode*. Episodes are then defined. The methodology for the division of the text into episodes is presented, and, finally, the grammatical and prosodic correlates of the episode boundaries are examined and analyzed.

Data

Data analyzed in this chapter come from a routine cholecystectomy operation which I observed and audiotaped. After the operation, I accompanied the resident, the medical student, and the patient to the Postanesthesia Recovery Room. Here, the patient was entrusted to the care of nurses, and a handwritten summary of the operation (see Appendix A) was written on the patient's progress notes. Following this, I accompanied the resident to the dictating area of the surgeons' lounge, and audiotaped his transcription of the operation. I later made a linguistically sensitive transcription of this dictation, including pauses and intonation (see Appendix J). A copy of the typed operative report was later collected (Appendix C), and the resident was interviewed approximately 1 month after the operation.

The resident who assisted at this operation and dictated the operative report had been in surgical residency training for 10 months at the time of the operation. This was the first time that he had had any real responsibilities in assisting in this particular procedure, and it was the first time that he had dictated a report of a cholecystectomy. The analysis in this chapter thus provides a baseline for a report of a first year resident to serve as an example in the Chapter 4 analysis.

Division of the Text as a Whole

A report of an operation, while it does contain a narrative section, differs from most narrative texts studied in discourse analysis. Most narrative texts contain information about the setting of the event and the participants in the event within the body of the narrative itself. In operative reports, however, such information is found outside the narrative part of the text, and is formatted on the page in various locations. (See Appendix C for the operative report examined in this chapter.) For example, a number of details of the setting, such as the date of the operation, and the hospital in which it was performed, along with the names of the participants, such as the patient, surgeon, and assistants, are not included in the narrative but are formatted in certain prescribed locations on the page. Some of this information is found in boxes on the text provided for this purpose; other information is provided in typewritten headings preceding the narrative section of the text.

Other information that is of bureaucratic, rather than medical, interest, which relates to the production of the text itself, is also located outside the actual narrative. The transcriptionist who typed the report, and the date of dictation and typing, are also not included within the body of the narrative. These types of information are formatted on the page in various locations as well.

Thus, we may conceive of two "macrolevels" of the text: (a) the formatting of information on the page, and (b) the "macrolevel" of subdivisions of the narrative section of the text.

In order to begin to analyze these texts and to come to an understanding of their macrostructure, I make two types of macrodivisions: (a) a division of the text as a whole as it appears on the page, and (b) a division of the narrative section of the procedure that was performed (the section that is labeled OPERATIVE TECHNIQUE is this report). First, let us proceed to the analysis of (a), the division of the text as a whole as it appears on the page.

Motivation for Division (a) is based on an examination of the layout of the text on the page, as indicated by capital letters and also by sections printed on the actual page. At the top of the page is found the name of the medical center, and underneath the name of the medical center is found *Medical Records Report*. Directly underneath this, the operative report is blocked off into four spaces, with headings for the following: (a) the patient's name, (b) patient's hospital number (which is the same as the Social Security Number in this hospital), (c) patient's room number, and (d) hospital. This medical center is comprised of five member hospitals, and the transcription for all the hospitals is done in one centralized office, so the name of the particular hospital where the operation was done is typed in this space.

Immediately below this line, nine sections are typed in capital letters: DATE OF OPERATION, SURGEON, ASSISTANTS, PREOPERATIVE DIAGNOSIS, POSTOPERATIVE DIAGNOSIS, OPERATION PER-

FORMED, ANESTHESIA, INDICATIONS FOR SURGERY, and OPER-ATIVE TECHNIQUE. The DATE OF OPERATION is the date that the surgery was performed. The SURGEON is the staff surgeon with operating privileges granted by the hospital who performed the operation and is legally responsible for it. At this hospital, most staff surgeons are also on the faculty of the School of Medicine. The next category, ASSISTANTS,[1] consists of any residents and medical students who may have been assisting in the operation. Resident assistants are graded into first and second assistants, depending upon the resident's level of training and the type of operation being performed. For example, a second year resident could be a first assistant for a cholecystectomy, but would rarely be granted the privilege to be first assistant on a complex carcinoma resection. In this particular operation, there were two assistants: a first year resident and a medical student. The resident has the title *Dr.* preceding his name, while the medical student does not. The medical student has the initials of the medical school he is attending, along with the Roman numerals *III*, thus indicating that he is a third year medical student.

Following this is the PREOPERATIVE DIAGNOSIS and POSTOPER-ATIVE DIAGNOSIS. Depending upon the course of the operation, the pre- and postoperative diagnoses may not necessarily be the same, although in this case they were. After that comes ANESTHESIA, where the type of anesthesia given is listed.

INDICATIONS FOR SURGERY is a section sometimes included in these reports (See also Chapter 1). Here, the surgeon dictating the operation gives a brief history and rationale for the patient being brought to surgery. The last subdivision is the OPERATIVE TECHNIQUE, where the actual narrative description of the operation is found.

At the bottom of the page are two lines for *signature*. The resident dictating the operative report may sign his or her name in the left-hand space, and the attending surgeon must authenticate the report; this is done in the right-hand space. At the very bottom of the report is another line of four blocks. The left hand block is a space for the date the operative dictation was done. Next to that is a section titled *Typed by*. Here the transcriptionist enters his or her identification number. To the right of that is *Date,* or the date transcribed. Finally, on the far right hand side is a space for *Type of report*. Here the transcriptionist types *O.R.* for an operative report, along with the page number of the report, in the case that the report is more than one page.

Some of the above categories such as the postoperative diagnosis and the

---

[1]In this case, resident and medical students were listed as assistants. In other cases, licensed surgeons may be assistants.

name of the primary surgeon and assistants are required by Joint Commission on Accreditation on Hospitals standards (1987).

The Report Narrative: Review of Literature on Episodes

My goal is to determine in a principled way the segmentation of the narrative position of this text into its parts. In analyzing this part of the report, I rely primarily on the literature of discourse analysis.

In analysis of a number of texts, which is the ultimate goal of the research here, we need to know the *plot* (Longacre 1976, Becker 1980) of the narrative section of this type of text. Plot is defined here as "a set of constraints on the selecting and ordering of episodes or motifs" (Becker 1980:226). In other words, we need to know what information is generally selected to be included in these reports and what is not, and then what the order of that information is.

In discourse analysis, it is commonly assumed that a text may be divided into an intermediate level above the sentence but below the level of the text itself. Such sections have been termed paragraphs (Longacre 1979, Hinds 1979), centers of interest (Chafe 1980), thematic paragraphs (Givon 1983), conceptual paragraphs (Lackstrom, Selinker, and Trimble 1973), and episodes (Longacre 1976, Becker 1980, van Diijk 1982). In general, this text based unit of episode is thought to be a semantic unit (Van Dijk 1982).

For this study, I have chosen to term these segments of text *episodes*, rather than paragraphs, as I feel that this term captures more closely the relationship of the surgical texts to their referents, the operations. That is, the sections of the surgery to which the episodes refer can be considered to be composed of "steps," and, in fact, are thought of this way by the surgeons themselves.[2] For example, a fifth year resident recalled how he learned to dictate these reports:

> Through the first couple months, I started reading the operative dictations, just to have some idea of what the other residents did and then I just did that step by step. I tried to make it into a cookbook. Step one is this, step two is this. And when I dictated, I wouldn't *say* "step one, step two" but that's what I was thinking in my mind.

A paragraph, to me, implies a typographic unit. The text examined in this chapter is typical of other such reports in that it is not divided into typographic units of paragraphs.

---

[2]For a discussion of similar phenomena in the psychological research literature, see Black and Boser (1979).

An episode, then, is defined in this study as that segment of the operative report which is considered to correspond to a step in the operation, as determined by a surgeon or resident. At present, it appears that each episode corresponds to one or more actions on a topic, e.g., "isolating the cystic artery," or "isolating the cystic duct and typing that."

The ease with which an analyst can determine the plot may depend on how *distant* (Becker 1980) the text is from the analyst. Becker points out that the work of the philologist (or discourse analyst) is "contextualizing conceptually distant texts" (1980:212). In other words, the analysis of a text requires the description of the relations between a text and its context. Such relations include the coherence between elements of the text, the relation of the text to other texts, the relation between the author and the readers or hearers of the text, and the relation between the text and its referent. Importantly, one such relationship of coherence is the constraints on selecting and ordering of episodes in the plot.

In describing these relations between a text and its context, I believe, however, that some texts are more "distant" from the analyst than are others. For example, in analyzing a very distant text, the analyst may be confronting a text from a language group different from that of the analyst's mother tongue; the culture from which the text comes may be quite far from that of the researcher; the text itself may be an inscribed version of a text that was once spoken; the text may have come from a historical period far from the present, and, furthermore, the analyst may have little familiarity with the text's referent. By the same token, a text may be close to the analyst. Here, the text would be from the same language and culture as that of the analyst; the text would be close to its original form (if the text had been spoken, the analyst would have an audio or videotape of the text, for example, or, if it had been written, then the analyst would be analyzing a written version of the text); the text would come from the recent present, and the analyst would have the text's referent close at hand. Needless to say, the analysis of most texts falls somewhere between these two poles of very distant and close.

In this study, I will first use the insights of those who analyze a "close" text. By this I mean that I try to get as "close" to one of these texts as possible. Since these texts are spoken (dictated) but are meant to be read, I observe, collect, and analyze the dictation (or spoken version) of the operative report. I also observe and audiotape the text's referent" the operation itself. In determining the plot and episodic structure of the spoken text, I interview the person who performed the surgery and ask him to segment the text into episodes. I examine the correspondences between the episode boundaries and structural phenomena such as lexis, syntax, and phonology.

All of these correlations are to gain some insight into the content (Linde

1983) of the plot. Linde states that, in discourse analysis, the choice typically exists between modeling content or modeling structure. Modeling structure, according to Linde, is much easier to model than content. Her intent in discourse analysis is to model structure and then model content to the extent that it is possible. But with this type of text where the referent, the surgery, is "distant" from me in that I am not a surgeon, I need to come to some understanding of the content of the plot and episodes or the unstated background knowledge that surgeons have when they produce the text in order to determine the structure. Then, from this indepth analysis of the spoken "close" text in this chapter, I procede to the analysis of the "distant" texts in subsequent chapters. In analyzing those operative reports, I obviously could neither observe the operations, since they occurred previously, nor could I interview their authors. In that part of the analysis, I utilize the insights of both the first analysis and of those discourse analysts who analyze more "distant" texts.

As stated, then, how an analyst goes about determining the episodes in a text depends, to some extent, on how "close" or "distant" the text is from the analyst. Of all the research literature discussing segmentation of texts,[3] I discuss in this section only those directly relevant to the research project underlying this study: Chafe (1980), van Diijk (1982), and Givon (1983). Chafe (1980), for example, analyzes "close" texts that are spoken. In *The Pear Stories* the experimenter showed a film to groups of subjects who then summarized the film orally to an interviewer. Chafe had not only the audiotaped versions of the texts, but also the texts' referent: the film. Therefore, the analyst is able to make use of intonational and pause phenomena in the segmentation of the texts into the intermediate level of text (or what Chafe terms "centers of interest").

van Dijk (1982) analyzes a written text that is slightly more distant than those analyzed by Chafe. The text analyzed is a news story, and so the text's referent is not as available for comparison with the text as are the Pear Stories. The criteria for segmentation into episodes in this analysis are claimed to be primarily semantic, but do appear to implicitly involve the analyst's understanding of the genre of Western journalistic news stories. Interestingly, both Chafe and van Dijk attempt to abstract from their empirical analysis and make claims about the nature of consciousness.

Givon (1983) analyzes more distant texts than do Chafe or van Dijk. Givon analyzes texts from non-Indo-European languages and cultures, which are generally inscribed from an oral text. In so doing, he is less

---

[3]There exists a fairly large body of research in the psychological literature of segmentation of action. Some representative references for the interested reader would be: Newtson (1973), Newtson and Engquist (1976), and Newtson, Engquist, and Bois (1977). For the segmentation of texts in surgery, none of these appear directly relevant.

inclined than is Van Dijk to rely implicitly on a knowledge of the culture, language or genre in the analyses. While the purpose of Givon's work is neither to determine episodic structure nor plot, his methodology for examining the movement of topics through the text can prove useful in examining episodic structure.

I will first describe the analyses of Chafe, van Dijk, and Givon, and then offer a critique of them. In analyzing a "close" text of an audiotaped spoken narrative of a film that was viewed, Chafe (1980) focuses on the relationship between consciousness ("the selective activation of small amounts of available information") (1980:xv) and the actual narrative produced. Chafe attempts to point out that there is a parallel between producing a narrative through time and the movement of consciousness through time. He first discusses smaller units (*idea units*) roughly equivalent to a clause, and then larger units (*centers of interest*). Each focus of consciousness, or piece of information which the subject chooses to narrate, is expressed through short spurts of language, which Chafe terms *idea units*. Idea units combine to make larger units of speech which are termed centers of interest. Thus, for example, in the following text, each line indicates an idea unit, and the complete segment is a *center of interest* (1980:28)

1. [1.15] A—nd [.1] then a boy comes by,
2. [.1] on a bicycle,
3. the man is in the tree,
4. [.9] and the boy gets off the bicycle,
5. and . . . looks at the man,
6. and then [.9] uh looks at the bushels,
7. and he . . . starts to just take a few,
8. and then he decides to take the whole bushel.

Criteria for identifying idea units are linguistic: intonation, (such as a rise or a fall in pitch,) pausing, and syntactic phenomena such as the tendency for each idea unit to correspond to a single clause and to begin with the word *and*. The length of these units are, according to Chafe, limited by built-in processing capabilities.

Chafe offers a rough typology of the way in which the idea units express focuses of consciousness, based on the functions of the focuses as parts of the "complete picture which is being communicated piece by piece" (1980:17). In the Pear Stories, most of the focuses of consciousness deal with people, descriptions of those people, and their actions. Some focuses of consciousness relate to the actual act of recall itself, such as discussion of memory processes, and personal interacation between the interviewer and interviewee. Additionally, some focuses are evaluations of the action (cf. Labov 1972) in which the speaker offers a judgment of some aspect of the action.

Centers of interest are the intermediate cognitive unit between idea units and a complete narrative. They are indicated by a distinctive falling intonation. This falling intonation frequently, but not always, corresponds to the end of a sentence. In fact, Chafe argues that it is the sentence final intonation rather than the syntactic end of a sentence that indicates that the speaker has achieved the end of a center of interest. In terms of meaning, "The achievement of the goal of some actions is what typically brings closure to an event sequence" (1980:28). Unlike focuses of consciousness which are governed by limitations in processing, centers of interest vary in length and complexity, and appear to be determined by judgments of the speakers and by learned schemas. In addition, length of centers of interest vary across speakers and within speakers at different times. Common centers of interest in the Pear Stories include settings, introductions of people and series of punctual events followed by a conclusion.

van Dijk (1982) analyzes a text that is slightly more distant than those analyzed by Chafe, in an attempt to contribute to a further definition of paragraph or episode from that previously found in the literature. He claims that this definition requires a characterization in terms of "semantic macrostructures." In so doing, van Dijk first points out the intuitive notions of an episode as being a part of a whole. For example, we can think of an "episode" in a movie, or an "episode" in our lives. Both the part and the whole involve sequences of events and actions. In an episode in life, then, we might think of "my trip to Europe." The semantic macrostructure under which the episode would be subsumed would be the label of "my trip to Europe." In essence, van Dijk argues that an "episode is a sequence of propositions that can be subsumed by a macroproposition" (1982:180).[4] The realization of an episode in the text is a sequence of propositions in the discourse.

The text that van Diijk analyzes is a *Newsweek* article entitled "Diplomacy: A New Team's Latin Text" from November 24, 1980. A section of the text follows:

(1) Nowhere will U.S. foreign policy change more abruptly — or radically — during the Reagan Administration than in Latin America. (2) And nowhere did the American election arouse greater passion. (3) Many governments in the region have breathed a sigh of relief at the prospect of Ronald Reagan in the White House. (4) In Chile last week Interior Minister Sergio Fernandez happily predicted that "the new United States Government will treat its friends as true friends," (5) and on a tour of several Latin American capitals, Chase Manhattan Bank chairman David Rockefeller told smiling audiences that

---

[4]This concept is quite similar to a "core generalization" (Lackstrom, Selinker, and Trimble 1973) in the English for Science and Technology literature.

Reagan would be a realistic President, that he would "deal with the world as he found it."

The analysis into espisodes is done in three steps. The goal is to segment the text into "nonreducible" macropropositions. In the first division into episodes, the "segmentation criteria" would be the level of description. For example, the analyst would examine the text and determine that (1) is a general thematic introduction about the USA; (2), a general thematic introduction about Latin America; and then (3) becomes more specific, describing the attitudes of the Latin American governments, and so on. We can see that, in this case, each episode would be roughly equivalent to a sentence.

The goal of the analysis, however, is to segment the text into "nonreducible" propositions. van Dijk notes that, for this particular text, there are changes in scene and/or changes in participants as the text changes from one episode to another. As a result, the episode change markers in many of the episodes are simply the first noun phrases, such as *many governments, In Chile,* etc.

In the end, then, the criterion for distinguishing one episode from another is that a subsequent proposition cannot be subsumed under the previous macroproposition. As a result, van Dijk's final segmentation results in three episodes for text analyzed: (1) is sentence (1): a general summary statement about USA foreign policy change in Latin America; (2) is sentence (2): also a general summary statement about reactions in Latin America to Reagan's election; and (3) is sentences (4)–(5): Latin American governments' relief.

Boundaries between one episode and another are significant in that they may be marked linguistically, not only by intonation (as noted by Chafe), but also by a number of other "grammatical signals" (van Dijk 1982:181).

1. Pauses and hesitation phenomena (fillers, repetition) in spoken discourse;
2. paragraph indentations in written discourse;
3. time change markers: *in the meantime, the next day*, etc. and tense changes;
4. place change markers: *in Amsterdam, in the other room*;
5. 'cast' change markers: introduction of new individuals (often with indefinite articles) or reintroduction of 'old' ones (with full noun phrases instead of pronouns);
6. possible word introducing or changing predicates (*tell, believe, dream*, etc.)
7. introduction of predicates that cannot be subsumed under the same (macro-) predicate, and/or which do not fit the same script or frame;
8. change of perspective markers, by different 'observing' participants or differences in time/aspect morphology of the verb (free) (in-) direct style.

van Dijk further notes that the first sentence of a new episode is often more general than subsequent ones in the episode.

Givon (1983) analyzes texts that are more distant than those analyzed by either Chafe or van Dijk. Givon's main focus is the study of continuity in discourse, and he sees three main types of continuity: continuity of theme, action, and topic. All three are interconnected in an episode (or, in Givon's term, *thematic paragraph*) in an implicational hierarchy:

continuity of theme > action > topics/participants

Thematic continuity, or what will be studied in the episodes in this study, is in some sense, the most difficult to specify. As Givon states:

> Thematic continuity is the overall matrix for all other continuities in the discourse. It is the hardest to specify, yet it is clearly and demonstrably there. Statistically, it coincides with topic and action continuity to quite an extent, within the thematic paragraph. The thematic paragraph is *by definition* about the same theme.

Thematic continuity is the most weakly coded in the grammar; according to Givon, it is coded by conjunction or clause coordination in a SVO language such as English.

Action continuity refers to both the sequence of actions in the episode and also to the adjacency of one action to another. Actions within an episode are usually given in the sequential order in which they occurred, and are primarily coded gramatically in verb tense, aspect, and/or modality.

The main focus of Givon's work, however, is an examination of the topics as they move through the text in narrative. Within episodes, then, can be found three major types of topics, according to their position in the episode. (a) *Chain initial topics* are typically newly introduced or newly reintroduced into the discourse, but are discontinuous from the preceding discourse context. If this topic is "important," it will probably continue. (b) *Chain medial topics* are continuous in terms of the preceding discourse context, but will not continue much further in the succeeding discourse. And (c) *Chain final topics* are usually continuous in terms of the preceding discourse context, but do not persist in the subsequent discourse.

Givon has worked out a numerical system fro tracking the movement of topics through a text. This system answers the demands of examination of a distant text, but this is not of concern here. The important concepts to remember at this point are the notions of the implicational hierarchy of theme, action, and topic continuity, and the types of topics found in episodes.

In summary, then, we can see that the notion of an intermediate level of text, somewhere between a sentence and the text itself, is a fairly well-established notion in discourse analysis. This unit, in general, is thought to be a semantic unit and can be subsumed under a macroproposition. The continuity of theme in an episode implies continuity of action and then of topics, according to Givon. Within an episode are found topics that are moving through the episode in various ways, be they newly introduced (chain initial), continuing (chain medial), or ending (chain final).

The movement from one episode to another requires a reorientation. This boundary between one episode and another may be marked by any or all of the following: (a) prosodic features such as a "sentence final intonation" (Chafe 1980), and/or pauses in a spoken text; (b) grammatical features, such as time change markers and place change markers; (c) introduction of new topics, and (d) a change in the level of generality of the first sentence of a new episode, among other things.

In general, then, the text-based unit of episode is thought to be a semantic unit. Within this unit is found a sequence of sentences which is about a certain theme. Moreover, it is not difficult to see that these semantic units are a "semantics based on an unacknowledged reliance on general knowledge" (Johnson-Laird 1983:369),[5] which also assumes stability of communicative purpose throughout the whole text, as Swales (personal communication, April 1, 1985) points out. For example, an analyst can fairly easily determine the macropropositions for a text such as that analyzed by van Dijk if that analyst is a member of the culture in which this text is produced and has some knowledge of Reagan foreign poilcy, Latin America, and the relationships between the two.

A similar problem exists in the way in which Chafe determines the end of a center of interest. Here, the end of a center of interest is seen to be the achievement of the goal of some action. While this may be fairly transparent to the analyst in a close text, in a more distant text, the goal of an action might not be so obvious.

Finally, one criterion for segmentation into episodes that van Dijk relies on heavily is the level of generality of the sections of the text. For example, in the Newsweek story, it is easy to see that "many governments in the region" is more general than is "Chile."

It is not my purpose to claim that these ways of determining macropropositions, achievement of a goal of an action, and the level of generality are invalid and therefore not useful because of the unacknowledged reference to real world knowledge by the analyst. On the contrary, such concepts will prove extremely useful to the analysis of this text and others in the database, once the world knowledge of the surgery itself has

---

[5]For a similar critique of determining macropropositions, see Brown and Yule (1983:110).

begun to be tapped. Recall that, earlier, I stated that, in this analysis, I attempt to model content to some degree in these texts, which are more or less opaque at this point. I do this in order to assist in determining structure. To rely only upon structure in segmenting the text at this point, or to attempt to determine the episodic structure based on real world knowledge, could result in an erroneous analysis. Note that, in the following segment of an operative report, it is difficult to determine the goal of the action or the level of generality of the information:

> A seven inch incision extending from the xiphoid process below the costal margin was made. This was extended down through the subcutaneous tissue to the anterior rectus sheath. The anterior rectus sheath was incised. The rectus abdominis muscle was incised using a knife. The peritoneal cavity was then entered. The incision was extended medial and lateral with Metzenbaum scissors. Next the abdominal cavity was explored and there were no abnormalities noted.

Similarly, to determine episodes by relying upon structural features alone would be equally misleading. For example, were we to rely upon structure in determining episode boundaries, we might conclude that the temporal adverbs *next* and *then* mark the boundaries. Without outside confirmation from a member of the speech community, however, who knows the world of the text, we would not be certain that these were, in fact, separate episodes. Thus, a methodology for analysis needs to be devised which taps the knowledge of informants from the speech community. The next section describes a first foray into an understanding of the content of the text.

Methodology for Determining Episodes

In order to lessen the obvious problems of the analyst attempting to determine the plot and episodic structure of the text, the resident who performed the operation and dictated the operative report was interviewed. This surgeon served as a specialist informant (Selinker 1979), in that he was asked, based on his professional expertise, to contribute to the analysis of the text. Following Huckin and Olsen (1983), this approach to the analysis of the text with the informant was more top-down than bottom-up, in that he was asked to perform a more macrolevel task of segmenting the text into steps rather than detailing more lower level grammatical and lexical features of the text. As with Huckin and Olsen, the author of the text rather than other specialist informant surgeons was chosen to aid in the analysis. In contrast to either of these studies, both written and spoken (transcribed with pauses and hesitation markers) versions of the text were presented to the informant for his commentary.

In this section, I describe that interview. First, the surgeon was shown the written version of the text, that is, a typewritten text. (See Appendix I. For simplicity of reference, I term the three texts discussed in this section Text 1, Text 2, and Text 3.) Text 1 was transcribed by the researcher from the surgeon's operative dictation. Text 1 is written in orthographic sentences, and is essentially similar in format to the narrative text section of any operative report that would be found on a patient's medical record. In fact, the only major difference between Text 1 and the narrative section of an operative report transcribed in the hospital is that Text 1 is double spaced rather than single spaced. The surgeon was asked, "If you could, read through this (Text 1) and mark for me or tell me where you think the different steps are for you."

Thus, on Text 1 are marked \/, which indicate episode boundaries that the surgeon noted. Additionally, as the surgeon read through Text 1, he commented on it and produced an oral account of the operation as well. This oral account is, in effect, a summary of the written text. (See Appendix K: Text 3.) The oral summary can also be considered to be the macropropositions of the episodes.

The surgeon was then shown the text in Appendix J, Text 2 (without the markings for episodes), after he had divided Text 1 into episodes. Text 2 is the version of the spoken text transcribed by the researcher. A sample of the text that he was shown is as follows:

(3.0) a
(2.0) seven inch incision extending
     (.) from the xiphoid process
     (.) below the costal margin
(1.0) was made. This was extended down through the
     (.) subcutaneous tissue
     (.) to the anterior rectal sheath. The anterior rectal sheath was incised
     (.) the
(2.0) rectus abdominis muscle was severed using a
(2.0) cautery
     (.) and the posterior rectus sheath was incised using
     (.) a knife. The peritoneal cavity was then entered.

Text 2 is a more precise, linguistically sensitive transcription of the surgeon's dictation. It is not written in orthographic sentences; rather, it is divided according to pauses noted on the dictation by the researcher. For example, (1.0) indicates a one second pause and begins a new string of words in the text. (.) indicates a short pause, generally one tenth of a second or less, and also begins a new string of words in the text. In addition, errors in dictation are kept in this version of the text.[6]

During this examination of Text 2, the surgeon further divided some episodes into subepisodes, and offered elaboration on some features of the text. In particular, in discussion of the subepisodes, he noted that "not all of them but a lot of them are actually separate mechanical steps." He also clarified in some places on the text where the pauses or breaks in the dictation correlated with his trying to remember details of the operation. Following this discussion, I have divided Text 2 into Episodes 1, 2, etc., and Subepisodes (10a), (10b).

For analysis, the surgeon's oral discussion of Text 1 and Text 2 have been combined into Text 3 (Appendix K). Text 3 consists of a separate page for each episode noted by the surgeon. Both the surgeon's oral discussion of the episodes and the linguistic transcription of the dictated operative report is on each page. For example, one episode of Text 3 is as follows:

Episode 4
"then exploration – exploration of the abdominal cavity"
　　　　　　　　The incision was extended
　　　(.) medial and lateral with
(1.0) Metzenbaum scissors.
(3.0) Next the abdominal cavity was explored
　　　(.) and there were no abnormalities noted except
　　　(.) adhesion to the anterior abdominal wall on the lower
　　　(.) portion of the abdominal cavity

Analysis

After gathering informant insights into the content of the episodes of this particular operative report, the text was examined to see if the boundaries between the episodes corresponded with any structural features of the text. In particular, I examine grammatical features such as temporal adverbs, prosodic features of pauses and intonation, and the level of generality of the initial sentence. Recall that one of the grammatical signals for episode boundaries is time change markers (van Dijk 1983). I first examine the temporal adverbs *next* and *then*, to determine if they correspond to episode boundaries.

The text was examined, and a fairly strong correspondence between episode boundaries as noted by the surgeon and the lexical items *next* and *then* were found. It is important to note, however, that there is not a one-to-one correspondence in all cases. In other words, without the

---

[6]Cf. Paget (1983) for a similar text display utilizing pauses as a unit of segmentation.

specialist informant's determining the episodes, an accurate division of the text would not be made if only the grammatical and prosodic features were examined. Note however, that, for the contrastive study in Chapter 4, this determination of episodes provides an initial heuristic. Obviously, each text examined in Chapter 4 could not be examined by a specialist informant.

In general, *next* was found: (a) to occur at the beginning of episode boundaries, and with first mention of frequently mentioned lexical items; and (b) to function as a switch reference between frequently mentioned lexical items. *then* was particularly interesting in that there was an alternation between (a) sentences with *then* preceded by a pause of at least (2.0), and (b) sentences in which *then* is not preceded by a pause. The former sentences correspond to the beginning of an episode or subepisode boundary; the latter do not. I discuss both later in this section. These analyses also point out some important features of the text.

Analysis of Next

1. *Next* corresponds to four episode boundaries noted by the surgeon: 5, 6, 7, and 8. These four episodes are found in the very center of the operative report. There are 11 episodes in all; four precede the above-mentioned, and three follow. We will see in the following discussion that one way of thinking about the episodic structure is similar to that proposed by Longacre (1976), in which the *peak* of a narrative, or, in the case of a procedural text, the target procedure to which the whole text is directed, is marked in a number of ways. Longacre offers the metaphor of the "crowded stage" as a way to think about this part of the text where the peak of the action is taking place. In a play, for example, at the height of the drama, often all the major participants are crowded onto stage and the climax of the drama is played out. This metaphor offers a way of thinking about this text. In the middle of the operation, after the abdomen has been opened, three major structures are manipulated:[7] the gallbladder, the cystic artery, and the cystic duct. In the operative report, there is a switch back and forth in the description of the manipulations on these three structures in Episodes 4, 5, 6, and 7. The *nexts* appear to be one grammatical means to keep these elements separated.

2. *Next* is found in two other places in the text, in Episodes 4 and 5, where they do not mark episode boundaries. (There are two *nexts* in Episode 5.) One of the *nexts*, in Episode 4, on further investigation with the surgeon, may correlate with an episode boundary. Another possibility, however, is

---

[7]In interviews with a number of residents, it was pointed out that these are the three major structures manipulated in this operation.

that it may be a textual representation of a difficulty in changing orientation when moving from one episode to another (Chafe 1979, 1980). I shall discuss both possiblities.

I include both Episodes 3 and 4 here. Note that the macroproposition for Episode 3 is "making the incision and getting into the abdominal cavity," and for Episode 4 is "exploration — exploration of the abdominal cavity":

(E3)

A seven inch incision extending from the xiphoid process below the costal margin was made. This was extended down through the subcutaneous tissue to the anterior rectal sheath. The anterior rectal sheath was incised. The rectus abdominis muscle was severed using a cautery and the posterior rectus sheath was incised using a knife. The peritoneal cavity was then entered.

(E4)

The incision was extended medial and lateral with Metzenbaum scissors. *Next* the abdominal cavity was explored and there were no abnormalities noted except adhesion to the anterior abdominal wall on the lower portion of the abdominal cavity.

In Episode 4, *next* might, upon further discussion with the surgeon, be found to correlate with a new episode boundary as well. In Episode 4, *next* is found in the second sentence. The macroproposition of the episode, as stated by the surgeon, is exploring the abdominal cavity. The macroproposition of the preceding episode is making the incision. The sentence which begins the episode appears, however, to relate more to Episode 3 than to 4, since it refers to the incision: "the incision was extended medial and lateral with Metzenbaum scissors." The following sentence in Episode 4 refers more to exploring the abdominal cavity: "*Next* the abdominal cavity was explored . . ." Thus, discussion of the incision, as found in the first sentence of the episode, might more appropriately be included in Episode 3, and further discussion with the surgeon could indicate that the episode does, in fact, begin with "*Next* the abdominal cavity . . ."

Another possibility, however, is that this place in the text corresponds to a reorientation from one part of the surgery to another. Chafe hypothesizes that "the among of difficulty in moving from one center of interest to the next increases with the amount of reorientation that is necessary — with the amount of change in background information. In other words, it is hard for a thinker/speaker to find a new center of interest in a new area where a new orientation in terms of space, time, people, and background activity is necessary" (1980:44).

A reading of Episode 3 shows that, prior to exploring the abdomen, some change in background information may have been necessary. Examining the text, we find that, first, an incision was made in the skin. Following this incision, cutting proceeds through the layers of tissue and muscle until "the peritoneal cavity was then entered." At this point, the incision itself was then extended. In other words, the surgeons at this point returned to the incision, made it larger, and then returned the abdominal contents in order to explore the abdomen. This indicates, perhaps, a point in the text where there was some cognitive difficulty (although not necessarily difficulty in the surgery itself) in reorientation from one part to another.

Without further discussion with a surgeon, I cannot say which possibility would be more plausible. The important thing to note at this point is, I believe, that there will be parts of these texts where a smooth transition from one episode to another is not likely.

The other instance of *next*, in Episode 5, was discussed with a surgeon and found definitely not to correspond to an episode boundary. Interestingly, however, there are two instances of *next* in this episode, rather than one, as in the other episodes. The text states in Episode 5: "*Next* the gallbladder was isolated using packs in the inferior portion below the liver to isolate the gallbladder. *Next* the Kocher was placed on the gallbladder and this was retracted . . ." The surgeon stated that the placing of the Kocher on the gallbladder and the retracting of it does not indicate a new episode; rather, it forms part of the general action of isolating the gallbladder. It may also be significant that, at the point between these two sentences, another surgeon entered the dictating room and began dialing and dictating his operative report. The surgeon studied here may well have lost his train of thought at this point. A (11.0) second pause exists here between these two sentences.

3. *Next* was also found to correspond to the first mention of two of the three most frequently mentioned lexical items in the text. Note that *next* corresponds to the introduction into the text of *the gallbladder* and *the cystic artery*, and, if we consider *next* in Episode 4 as an episode boundary, *abdominal cavity*.

In this text, there are 53 NPs which refer to structures in the operation, whether anatomic structures, instruments, or sutures. Of these 53, *gallbladder*, is the most frequently mentioned of all NPs in the original dictated text. Gallbladder is mentioned 11 times, including one mention of *the neck of the gallbladder* and two of *the base of the gallbladder*, as well as one mention which was an error in dictation. *Next* also corresponds to the first mention of the *cystic artery* (five instances, including *this* and *the artery*.) The *abdominal cavity* was mentioned three times in the text.

Other lexical items mentioned frequently in the text include: the cystic duct (6), the patient (4), the anterior rectus sheath (3), and Metzenbaum scissors (3). None of the first mentions of these lexical items cooccurs with either temporal adjective *next* or *then*.

4. *Next* functions as a switch reference, to reintroduce lexical items which were not mentioned in either the previous episode or in preceding subepisodes. Note, for example, in Episode 7, that *the base of the gallbladder* had been mentioned in Episode 5, but not in Episode 6. *Next* functions somewhat similarly as a switch reference in Episode 8 in reintroducing *the gallbladder* into the text. Although *the base of the gallbladder* had been mentioned in Episode 7a, Episode 7 was considered to consist of three subepisodes. Both Subepisodes 7b and 7c dealt with the cystic duct rather than with the gallbladder. Thus, when the referent again becomes *the gallbladder* in Episode 8, it is found to cooccur with *next*.

Analysis of Then

Then also corresponds to some episode boundaries as does *next*.[8] The question arises whether each temporal adverb performs the same or different functions in the text. In this section, a careful examination will be made of the distribution of *next* and *then*, taking into account the resident's segmentation of the text into episodes, and the prosodic feature of pauses. In so doing, the alternation between *next* and *then* provides an indication of deeper, more significant phenomena related to the surgery itself.[9]

In this section, I question why this resident uses two rather than one temporal adverb in the text. I have shown in the above that *next* is at the beginning of an episode boundary in most cases. Those episodes were generally in the center of the text — the place where the anatomic structures that are most crucial to the operation are manipulated. *Next* also corresponded to first mention or reintroduction of these important topics.

The question arises of why another temporal adverb, *then*, should be in the text, and also why *then* is sometimes found at the end of an episode and sometimes at the beginning. In the examination of the alternation between *next* and *then*, the additional dimension of pauses and intonation enters into the analysis. When we examine the *then* sentences, we find there is an alternation between the *then* sentences with and without pauses. A further question arises regarding the above distribution of this additional alternation. In this section, I explore these questions about *then*.

In contrast to *next* sentences (which are *all* preceded by pauses), in *then*

---

[8]Some observations on *then* and the level of generality of the verb come from a discussion with Richard Frankel.

[9]Cf. Tomlin and Rhodes (1979) and Pettinari (1983) for discussion of grammatical alternations.

sentences, there is an alternation between (a) sentences with the temporal adverb preceded by hesitations too brief to be counted (*Then hesitation sentences* or THS), and (b) sentences with the temporal adverb preceded by a pause of at least (2.0) (*then pause sentences,* or TPS). (For a further discussion of prosodic features of pauses and intonation, see the following section.) While *next* plus a pause indicated an episode boundary, it is important to note that the *combination* of *then* and a pause is indicative of an episode boundary, but that *then* without a pause is not.

Examining the alternation between THS and TPS offers one way of examining both the different textual functions of *then* and the syntagmatic relationship between *next* and *then* in this text. I claim here that *next* and *then* are not used interchangeably. Quirk and Greenbaum (1973:287) conflate the textual functions of *next* and *then*:

> There is a corresponding series of adjuncts with *first* (also *at first* and, less commonly, *firstly*) as the beginning of the set; *next, then, later, afterwards,* as interchangeable middle terms; and *finally, lastly,* or *eventually* as markers of the end of the set.

An examination of *then* in the context of surgical and other texts demonstrates two textual functions. *Then* can indicate one in a series of actions and/or, the result of the preceding actions. In order to illustrate these dual functions of *then*, consider the following example from a *New Yorker* article about the presidential debates (Drew 1984:156):

> In the course of their argument over Reagan's proposal to develop a defensive anti-missile system — his "Star Wars" proposal — Reagan committed two gaffes. First, he said that he would give the Soviet Union a "demonstration" of such a system in order to persuade it to join in constructing one. He went on to say that all nuclear weapons could then be eliminated, because both sides would feel secure.

Here, the sentence with *then* has dual characteristics. The first characteristic (the *series* characteristic) is that it is second in a series of two things: Reagan's gaffes. The series is marked linguistically in the text as *first* and *then*. The other characteristic of *then* is that what is being talked about is the *result* of the preceding actions (the *result* characteristic). Here, *then* refers back to preceding actions in the text (a backreference) (Jespersen 1964), and is the logical result of these actions. In other words, the information following *then* is a conclusion to the preceding actions. So we see here that the elimination of nuclear weapons could be (to Reagan's mind, at least) the *result* of demonstrating the weapons system to the Russians. The *then* sentence is not only second in a series of two items, but, more importantly for this discussion, it indicates the result of the preceding action.

A similar phenomenon may occur in the surgical text under investigation. *Then* can indicate both a series and/or a result. Let us look at the THS sentences which I claim indicate a result. They all occur at the *end* of episodes. For example, consider Episode 3, which is "making the incision and getting into the abdominal cavity." In this episode, a number of structures are cut through in order to enter the abdominal cavity:

(E3)

A seven inch incision extending from the xiphoid process below the costal margin was made. This was extended down through the subcutaneous tissue to the anterior rectal sheath. The anterior rectal sheath was incised. The rectus abdominis muscle was severed using a cautery and the posterior rectus sheath was incised using a knife. *The peritoneal cavity was then entered.*

We can see that the incision was made, extended down through one structure, the subcutaneous tissue, to another: the anterior rectal sheath. Then three more structures were incised: the anterior and posterior rectus sheath and the rectus abdominis muscle. As a *result* of these actions, the peritoneal cavity was entered. Or consider another THS:

(E6) "isolating the cystuic artery."

Next the cystic artery was dissected free and a 2-0 vicryl suture was passed around the cystic artery. This was ligated and a second 2-0 vicryl suture was placed again around the cystic artery. *The artery was then ligated between the two sutures.*

In this episode, two sutures were placed around the cystic artery. It appears that the final and resulting act was ligating the cystic artery between the two sutures.

Then also occurs at the end of Episode 5: "starting the bulk of the operation—isolating the gallbladder." The use of *then* to signal a result (at least in the first independent clause) is not quite as obvious as in the previous two examples.

(E5)

Next the gallbladder was isolated using packs in the inferior portion below the liver to isolate the gallbladder. Next the Kocher was placedon the gallbladder and this was retracted so that the neck of the gallbladder could be seen. *The cholecystoduodenal ligament was then incised and the base of the gallbladder was isolated.*

However, it may be part of a surgeon's technical knowledge that incising the cholecystoduodenal ligament is the logical result of the preceding actions. The above examples are *then* hesitation sentences — sentences which are preceded by only slight hesitations in the dictation and which occur at the end of the episodes.

It is significant to note that, with the latter two episodes discussed (Episodes 6 and 5), each subsequent episode begins with *next* and a new or reintroduced topic is brought into the discourse. Thus, *next* and *then* are not used interchangeably in this text.

I now go on to discuss those three episodes or subepisodes in which the initial sentence begins with *then* (or TPS): 9 (tying the cystic duct), and 10 and 10a(closing the abdominal cavity). Episode 9 contained errors in the dictation; the surgeon backtracked and changed his wording. Therefore, I will not discuss it here. However, the *then* sentences in Episode 10 will be discussed. I claim that one of these sentences (in E10a) has the function of indicating *both* a series and a result, and the other (in E10d) indicates only a series. These differences correspond, not only to the pauses, but also to the location of *then* in the sentence.

I would like to point out the position that *then* can have in a sentence: either initial or following the subject. The position of *then* in the sentence may indicate whether the series or result function is being employed. Let us first examine the syntagmatic relationship between *next* and *then* in the following examples:

(1a) I went into the kitchen.
      Next I found a cookbook.
      Then I made cookies.
(1b) I went into the kitchen.
      Next I found a cookbook.
      I *then* made cookies.
(1c) I went into the kitchen.
      Then I found a cookbook.
      Next I made cookies.

In (1a) and in (1b), the final sentences are marked with *then* and are the result of the preceding two actions: going into the kitchen and finding a cookbook. The difference between (1a) and (1b) is that *then* in (1a) is in initial position and in (1b) it follows the subject. *Then* in (1a) appears to have more of a flavor of being one in a series of actions than does *then* in (1b). (1c) seems slightly incongruous; *next* seems as though it should introduce a new type of action and/or topic.

These examples roughly show that *then* appears to be the next logical step in a series of actions, and the action in the *then* sentence could not have occurred without the preceding actions. Also, if *then* is in initial position, it appears to indicate one of a series of actions; if *then* occurs within the body of the sentence, it may have the dual function of indicating both a series and the result of the preceding actions (as in the *New Yorker* text.)

Let us now return to examine Episode 10: "finally closing the abdominal cavity." Thinking of E10 as a mirror image of E3 ("making the incision and getting into the abdominal cavity") is helpful in examining the textual functions of *then* in two ways. The actions in these episodes of the operation are mirror images of one another, and, also, the *then* sentences appear to be like mirror images. In Episode 3, a number of structures were cut to enter the abdominal cavity, and in Episode 10, those structures were sutured back together to close the abdominal cavity.

(E3)

A seven inch incision extending from the xiphoid process below the costal margin was made. This was extended down through the subcutaneous tissue to the anterior rectal sheath. The anterior rectal sheath was incised. The rectus abdominis muscle was severed using a cautery and the posterior rectus sheath was incised using a knife. *The peritoneal cavity was then entered.*

(E10)

The abdominal cavity was then irrigated using normal saline. Hemostasis was obtained and the abdominal wall was closed. *First* the posterior rectus sheath was closed using 2-0 vicryl suture. *Then* the anterior rectus sheath was closed using 2-0 vicryl suture. The subcutaneous tissue was closed using 3-0 vicryl and the skin was closed using staples.

These underlined *then* sentences appear to be virtual mirror images of one another. E3 *ends* with a *then* sentence, "The peritoneal cavity was then entered," but E10 *begins* with a *then* sentence, "The abdominal cavity was then irrigated using normal saline." Both of these sentences have the resultative character of being the conclusion of the preceding actions. In Episode 3, the sentence ends the episode, because all of the structures are cut and then the surgeon is able to enter the abdomen.

In Episode 10, the first *then* sentence is a result of preceding actions as well. But these actions (taking out the gallbladder, tying the cystic duct and artery) occurred in the preceding *episodes* rather than in the preceding sentences, as in E3. In Episode 10, following these actions, the abdominal cavity was cleaned out ("The abdominal cavity was *then* irrigated using normal saline") and the structures that had been cut in ED3 were put back together in E10. But note here that this TPS sentence *begins* the next episode. The subsequent actions that are expressed in Episode 10 are the separate mechanical procedures involved in closing the abdomen. Thus, the first *then* sentence functions as both a resultative sentence, in that it refers back to the preceding actions and is the end result of the preceding actions, and as a series, in that it indicates the beginning of the next episode.

The second *then* sentence in the episode, however, is somewhat different. It is second in a series of actions: *first* the posterior rectus sheath was closed; *then* the anterior rectus sheath was closed. Here, *then* is in the initial position in the sentence; thus, it marks an action in a series of other actions.

These particular *then* sentences in E3 and E10 are not the only examples of mirror images that we see here. On a larger scale, the actions expressed in the verbs in the THS and TPS appear to mirror one another too. The following are lists of the verbs found in the *then hesitation sentences* and the *then pause sentences* along with the episodes in which they occur.

THS	TPS
(E3) entered	
(E5) incised	(E9) tied
(E6) ligated	(E10a) irrigated
	(E10d) closed

It is interesting to note that the actions move from entering the peritoneal cavity (which is an action expressed in general terms), to incising (or cutting), and then ligating. In E9, the verb is tying (which is similar in meaning to "ligating") and then irrigating. Finally, in E10d, the verb is *closed*; that is to say, almost the complete opposite of *entered*.

Prosodic Features and Episode Boundaries

While the temporal adverbs *next* and *then* do correspond to the beginnings and/or endings of episode boundaries, the prosodic features of sentence final intonation (Chafe 1980) and pauses do not correspond quite so clearly. Although the presence of pauses *along with* grammatical signals correspond to episode boundaries, in and of themselves they do not signal episode boundaries. Recall that Chafe (1980), indicated that sentence final intonation indicated the end of a center of interest. In Chafe's terms, such centers of interest are a single mental image; when the subject judges that he or she has achieved adequate communication of the image, the sequence is completed with a sentence final intonation.

In the text under investigation here, while sentence final intonation is found at the end of eight of the eleven episode boundaries (E1-2, E4-6, E8-10), it is also found *within* episodes in 13 other locations as well. As an example, we see sentence final intonation in E5 occurring at the end of one sentence within the episode and at the end: (, = rising intonation, . = falling). This episode is laid out using Chafe's format.)

(E5)
1. (4.0) Next the gallbladder was isolated,
2. using (.) packs in the (3.0) inferior portion (.) below the liver,
3. to isolate the gallbladder,
4. (11.0) next the Kocher was placed on the gallbladder,
5. and this was retracted,
6. (.) so that the neck of the gallbladder could be seen.
7. The cholecystoduodenal ligament,
8. was then incised,
9. and the base of the gallbladder was isolated.

It is clear, then, that there is some difference between centers of interest as expressed by Chafe and episodes in this text. It appears that what, for Chafe, is a center of interest correlates, in the end, exclusively with a sentence final intonation. There is no place in Chafe (1980) where a center of interest is *longer* than an intonational sentence, by definition or by coincidence. In other words, a center of interest is *only* an intonational sentence, according to Chafe's analysis.

In the text under investigation here, however, an episode as defined by the surgeon may consist of more than one action, if that action relates to the macroproposition given. It may be that an episode consists of more than one center of interest. However, for comparative purposes later in this study, I prefer to rely on the informant's judgment about the content of an episode.

A similar problem exists with the other prosodic feature of pauses. Again in this text, many pauses are found within the episodes as well as at the episode boundaries (cf. E5 above). Although Chafe mentions pauses only briefly in his 1980 paper, a 1979 paper dealing with the same data notes that pauses correspond to what he terms episode boundaries. The relationship between episodes in Chafe (1979) and (1980) are not clear.

No doubt one explanation for the many pauses in the text is that the surgeon dictating it is a first year resident who is producing this type of report for the first time, and he may be having trouble remembering the steps or what to include in the steps. In fact, this resident told me that "when you start out you have enough trouble remembering the routine things that go in every normal operation." He further elaborated on places in the text where he paused to think of how many or what types of sutures were used. In other words, in a technical text such as this, there may be contextual factors such as another person entering the dictating room, or memory, or technical factors such as those mentioned above to account for the pause pattern in this text that would not be found in the type of experimental design as that in Chafe (1979, 1980).

Level of Generality of the First Sentence in Episodes

The last correlate of episode boundaries to be discussed here is the level of generality of the first sentence in the episode. Recall that van Dijk (1982) observed that the first sentence of a new episode is often more general than subsequent ones in the episode. While, again, this may be fairly transparent in texts where we share world knowledge with the world of the text, in these operative reports, it is somewhat difficult to discern the level of generality of the sentences.

I hypothesize that the level of generality in the first sentence is indicated both by the verb and also (in some cases) by the presence of two arguments following the verb: the instrument and locative. At this point, I will discuss this phenomenon in only a rather general and intuitive way, as does van Dijk. However, I will point out what I see in the text. (Table 3.1) is an abstract of the sentences in the text. Only Episodes 3 through 10 are given, as they are the parts where the surgeon is actually within the patient's abdomen. I have included the topic of the sentence, the verb (*was* is omitted in this table after the first sentence, although, of course, *was* is in the text before each verb), and then the arguments following the verb. Instrument is abbreviated as *I*, and locative is abbreviated as *L*. Verbs that are in italics are the verbs that I consider to be more "general" than others.

Two observations are worth noting here: the level of generality of the verb, and the number of arguments following the verb. First, the initial sentences in the episode tend to have verbs that are more "general" than are other verbs in the episodes. Note E3, for example. The first verb is *made*. This verb does not indicate a precise type of manipulation as do other verbs in the episode such as *incised* or *severed*, both of which are types of cutting. Similarly, in E4 and E5, the verbs in the first sentences are *dissected free*, which seems to indicate both the action of cutting and also cutting away from something and freeing it. *Dissected free* seems to me to indicate more general types of movements than do *passed, ligated,* or *placed,* each of which appear to indicate only one manipulation. Similarly, in E8, *freed* also shows an action that is resultative rather than descriptive.

The combination of both arguments of instrument and locative occur *only* in the first sentences of episodes. Other sentences within episodes may have combinations of two instruments or two locatives, but not one of each. Interestingly, those initial sentences with the arguments of both instrument and locative are both about the gallbladder. For example, in E5, "The

Table 3.1.   Level of Generality of Verb

Topic	Verb	Instrument or Locative
(E3)		
incision	was *made*	
this	was extended down through L to L	
ant. reactus sheath	incised	
rectus abdominis	severed	using I
post. rectus sheath	incised	using I
peritoneal cavity	*entered*	
(E4)		
incision	extended	with I
abdominal cavity	explored	
no abnormalities	noted	except _____
(E5)		
gallbladder (GB)	isolated	using I in L to (purpose)
Kocher	placed	on L
this	retracted	so that (purpose)
neck of the GB	could be seen	
cholecystoduodenal ligament	incised	
base of the GB	isolated	
(E6)		
cystic artery	*dissected free*	
2–0 vicryl suture	passed	around L
this	ligated	
second 2–0 vicryl suture	placed	around L
the artery	ligated	between I and I
(E7)		
base of the GB	*dissected free*	using I
cystic duct	(ligated)	(error in dictation)
cystic duct	isolated	using I
2–0 silk tie	placed	around I
(E8)		
GB	*freed*	from L using I
entire GB	free	from L
(0)	attached	to L by L
(E9)		
cystic duct	tied	
cystic duct	ligated	
GB	to be removed	
(E10)		
abdominal cavity	irrigated	using I
hemostasis	*obtained*	
abdominal wall	*closed*	
post. rectus sheath	*closed*	using I
ant. rectus sheath	*closed*	using I
subcutaneous tissue	*closed*	using I
skin	*closed*	using I

gallbladder was isolated using packs in the inferior portion below the liver to isolate the gallbladder," and in E8, "The gallbladder was freed from the liver bed using blunt dissection and Metzenbaum scissors." The above suggests that the level of generality of the initial sentence may be indicated in the verb in this particular text. Furthermore, sentences with both arguments of instrument and locative are found *only* in initial sentences in episodes.

Conclusion

In this chapter, a methodology is proposed that takes into account the several texts that produce the final orthographic text. The spoken and written texts are collected. The resident who dictated the operation is interviewed in order to determine how he would divide the text into steps. In so doing, he produced a summary, or the macropropositions, of each episode. Thus, in the analysis, all of the data collection points — spoken dictated text, written text, and specialist informant interview — are made transparent, and each informs the other in various ways. This methodology provides a thick description (Geertz 1973) of the text which not only interprets the text, but also works back through its construction in the analysis. The findings of the analysis are summarized in the following pages.

In this chapter, I have shown that there are two macrolevels in this particular text: (a) the formatting of certain information outside the narrative summary of the operation itself, including identification data of the patient, surgeons, type of operation and pre- and postoperative diagnoses, along with information central to the dictation and transcription of the report; and (b) the episodic structure of the narrative summary.

Some general observations may be made about this particular text based on the macropropositions noted by the surgeon, the analyses of *next* and *then*, and the level of generality of some of the initial sentences in the episodes. These observations will form the basis from which to proceed to the contrastive analyses of the data base in succeeding chapters.

(1) This text may be analyzed into 11 episodes. The first two episodes (E1) and (E2) and the last (E11) deal with preparation of the patient for surgery in the former, and the patient's condition on termination of the surgery in the latter. Episode 3 details the structures cut into in order to reach the gallbladder, and, in E10, those structures are closed back together. Consequently, in this text, E3 and E10 are mirror images of each other, both in the way in which the structures manipulated mirror each other, and also in the presence of a *then* sentence at the end of E3 and at the beginning of E10. The episodes which are found in the middle of the text are also central in the performance of the operation. These episodes involve exploration of the

abdominal cavity (E4) and then the technical procedures followed in taking out the gallbladder (E5–E9).

(2) In general, an episode consists of one or more actions on a topic. Some examples include "exploration of the abdominal cavity," "isolating the gallbladder," or "isolating the cystic artery."

(3) In this particular text, many episode boundaries are marked by the temporal adverbs *next* and *then*. *Next* corresponds to the beginning of the four central episodes: E5, E6, E7, and E8. These are the episodes in which the structures important to the operation are manipulated: the gallbladder, cystic artery, and cystic duct. *Next* occurred with first mention or reintroduction of two of these structures: the gallbladder and the cystic artery. It was also suggested that, in some places in the text, reorientation from one episode to another takes place over more than one sentence.

Then was determined to have two functions in this text: (a) to indicate the result of some preceding actions, and (b) to indicate the result of some preceding actions. The textual function (b) corresponded with the prosodic feature of pause in the text as well as, in one case, of *then* being in initial position in the sentence rather than following the subject.

(4) The verb in the first sentence in many episodes tended to be more "general" than other verbs in the episodes. By this I mean that more than one manipulation may be subsumed by the meaning of the verb. Furthermore, the first sentences of episodes are the only place in the text where both instrument and locative are found in one sentence.

In following chapters, I examine the episodic structure of many texts of the same type of operation performed by several different surgeons at different levels of training, and thereby begin to obtain an understanding of the constraints on the selecting of information within the episodes.

CHAPTER 4

CHANGE IN REPORTING STYLES OF SURGICAL RESIDENTS

Introduction

Surgical residents contend that, as they develop through residency training, their operative reports change. In particular, residents believe that these reports become "more detailed, briefer, and more likely to be in proper order." By "detailed" I believe they mean "appropriately detailed" for the purposes of the report (cf. Garfinkel 1967). During the course of their training, residents come to learn that some information need be reported on in greater detail than other information. In other words, as they proceed in training, resident surgeons begin to get a sense of what information can be inferred by the likely audience for these reports, and what cannot (see Chapter 1 for a typology of audiences for these reports), as well as an understanding of what information is needed for future patient care purposes.

In this section, I explore the notion of "detailed" and where in the reports it is crucial to include more extensive detail. In so doing, I show a subtle shift in the way in which residents produce this type of text from the beginning to the end of their residency training. The shift is from a text which details the narration of a procedure to a text which becomes more of a descriptive enumeration: parts of the patient's anatomy are described in greater detail, and the narration of the procedure, although still present, is consolidated. In other words, the relative "weight" of the text in the beginning is toward describing the procedure performed, and in the end is toward describing the findings.

As an example to show how the reports become less narrative in their focus, I present one fifth year resident's beliefs of how his reports differed between the beginning and end of residency training:

> I found out that I was being too *tech*nical, you know. I was—'the subcutaneous tissues were cut with a Metzenbaum scissors' and 'fine hemostats were used to clamp the blood vessels and tie individi . . .'. You don't need to say all that. You just say 'hemostasis was obtained' you know. And then you go on, cut out a lot of the fat.

The analysis in this chapter shows that this intuition holds true for the difference in reporting styles. Let us examine two sentences from the above examples which report on one particular procedural part of the operation: obtaining hemostasis. (Hemostasis is defined as "arrest of bleeding or of circulation;" a hemostat is "a device or medicine which arrests the flow of blood" (Taber 1962:H-27). For example, note the contrast between the following:

1. Fine hemostats were used to clamp the blood vessels and tie individi
   . . .
2. Hemostasis was obtained.

Sentence (1) describes an action; (2) indicates the resulting state following the performing of an action. We can infer from this example that, for the purposes of this type of reporting, it appears sufficient to know that the state of controlled bleeding was achieved rather than the detail of the process of controlling that bleeding. This resident apparently considers a number of details extraneous to this particular procedure, then, such as the type of instrument used to control bleeding, the verb "were used" which indicates an action performed by the surgeon to a fairly close degree, and the two separate actions of clamping the vessels and tying. While there is no doubt that (1) is more "detailed," the level of detail deals with delineating the separate steps of this particular procedure, along with naming the instrument that accomplishes the actions involved to carry out the procedure. In other words, in (1), the action could almost be replicated. Such detail may obviously be inferred by the surgeon reader of operative reports. Much other information, needless to say, is not inferrable, at least by another surgeon who may need to read these reports for further patient care in the event of a contingency.

Some analogies may be helpful in considering the difference between the first year reports and the fifth year reports. One is that given by Hofstadter (1979),[1] who argues that we can understand a thing at different "levels of

---

[1] I thank John Lawler for pointing out the relevance of Hofstadter and deGroot's studies to this one.

description;" in our perception of things, we can shut off some things and pay attention to others. For example, Hofstadter points out that, if we are watching an actress on a television, we know that we are not actually looking at a woman, but at flickering images on the screen. We can shut out one representation, the flickering dots, and pay attention to others, the woman. As an example of the ability to selectively organize attention to various levels of phenomena, Hofstadter refers to a study (de Groot 1965) which examines how chess "novices" and chess "masters" perceive a chess situation. In looking ahead to what move to make, the master sees the distribution of pieces on the board in *chunks* rather than as a series of moves. In reproducing the actual position in a game, the master could reproduce a position with rapidity, compared with the novice's "plodding reconstruction of the game." Hofstadter (1979:286) concludes that:

> The conclusion is that in normal chess play, certain types of situation recur — certain patterns — and it is to those high-level patterns that the master is sensitive. He thinks *on a different level* from the novice; his set of concepts is different.

I would argue that this analogy is helpful in understanding the difference between the first and final reports, although the terms "novice" and "master" may be somewhat misleading in that they imply a judgment of the residents' abilities. When residents approach the task of reporting, they, too, must selectively attend to some phenomena and not to others. I suggest that, in organizing information for reporting purposes, beginning residents observe the operation as a series of moves, or steps, that need to be reported on, and the resident does not necessarily have the experience to filter out some things and pay attention to others in the reporting. The fifth year residents, on the other hand, have had more experience with the "recurring patterns" of various types of operations, including information needed for future reference. In the act of reporting on an operation, they then, no doubt, selectively organize their attention to those levels of description.

The professor of surgery who has served as a specialist informant to this project confirms that these differences conform to his intuitions about residents' reporting. In fact, he questioned whether these perceptions of what is marked and unmarked in an operation, for reporting purposes, can be taught to beginning residents. At present, this is an open-ended question. I believe it will be tested empirically with applied linguistics research.

Another way of thinking about the difference between certain features of the beginning and final reports examined in this chapter is that of "writer-based prose" vs. "reader-based prose" (Flower 1981). Writer-based prose is organized according to a logic based on the writer's own needs. Frequently, writer-based prose is recognizable in particular by an egocentric focus on the writer and a narrative organization focused on the writer's own discovery process. Reader based prose, on the other hand, is focused around information that readers want to obtain. While operative reports could be designed more radically so that true reader-based elements would be highlighted (see Chapter 5), the final reports examined in this chapter do contain more elements of information that fifth year residents consider important to include.

In this chapter, I first show that the narrative section[2] of these operative reports is the result of two language acts: describing the procedure that was performed, and describing the observations that the surgeon made about the patient's anatomy during the operation. I then examine the kinds of information that fifth year residents consider important to include in operative reports of cholecystectomies. These elements are termed *criteria* (Payne 1979), and beginning and final reports of all five fifth year residents in this training program are examined against their criteria, which are divided into a description of the procedure and a description of findings. The first and last operative reports of cholecystectomies dictated by these residents are examined against the criteria, and I show that, while fifth year residents' reports contain more information relevant to both the procedure and findings, a somewhat larger increase is found in information describing the findings. I then discuss the rhetorical differences between texts that describe an essentially temporal dimension, such as a procedure, as opposed to a spatial dimension, such as observations. Finally, I show how these differences come to be reflected, not only in the kinds of information found in first and last reports of this data base, but also in the rhetorical, grammatical, and lexical features of these texts.

Two Language Acts: Describing the Procedure and Describing the Findings

In examining change over time, I have considered it important to examine changes that occur in the actual content recorded on the reports, as well as the rhetorical and linguistic style of the reports. It will be established that residents report on different kinds of information at the beginning and at the end of residency training. It will also be established that they move the focus of reporting from rhetorical acts of describing procedures to describ-

---

[2]The use of the term *narrative* here may be confusing. *Narrative section* of the report is the part of the report where the surgeon describes what was done during the surgery, as opposed to other sections of the text, e.g., (a) Indications for Surgery, and (b) the beginning section, which lists the surgeons, pre and postoperative diagnoses, etc.

ing findings.[3] It is then hypothesized that, as a result, the linguistic features of the text that stem from those language acts change as well.

In order to examine change in information recorded on the reports, I first chose to determine what information the fifth year residents considered important to be included[4] in their reports. Criteria (Payne 1979)[5] of information considered important to include were developed in interviews with the residents. In developing these criteria, I asked the fifth year residents interviewed, and the professor of surgery, "What information is important to include in these (cholecystectomy) reports?" and "Which steps in the operation do you think are important to focus on in your reporting?"[6]

---

[3]Motivation for considering that these reports consist of the language acts of describing procedures and describing findings come from two sources: from the standards set forth by the Joint Commission on Accreditation of Hospitals (JCAH), and from an observation made by an assistant professor of surgery. These standards regarding operative reports state that "operative reports . . . should contain *a description of the findings, the technical procedures used,* (emphasis mine) the specimens removed, the postoperative diagnosis and the name of the primary surgeon and any assistants" (Joint Commission on Accreditation of Hospitals 1987:100). The professor of surgery, in discussing the kinds of surgery performed by junior (first and second year) residents, noted that "the kinds of surgery that junior residents do (e.g., "lumps and bumps," surface biopsies, inguinal hernias and cholecystectomies) does not test their descriptive skills."

[4]Cf. discussions in Douglas and Pettinari (1983) and Bley-Vroman and Selinker (1984) and about establishing important information in texts with specialist informants for English for Specific Purposes research and pedagogy.

[5]Establishing criteria of information considered essential to document the quality of care in the medical record can be a part of hospital medical auditing and quality assurance activities. The purpose of criteria development is to establish measures to evaluate and measure clinical performance. See Lyons and Payne (1974) and Payne (1979) re criteria development in evaluating individual and group performance in auditing medical practice. See also Goldstein and Way (1978) on criteria development in medical auditing as a teaching tool in surgical education. It is important to note that the above criteria development examines the entire medical record. To my knowledge, criteria have not yet been developed for information to be included on the operative report in the medical record, although protocols have probably developed for pathology reporting (Payne, personal communication, January 29, 1985), another medical speciality. As these criteria in this chapter have not been developed in as detailed a fashion as is done in medical auditing (e.g., no census of experts have been obtained, no contingency items such as age or severity of disease determined, norms have not been established as to the level of conformity to the criteria, criteria have not been weighted as to how relatively important each are), in no way should these criteria in this chapter be considered evaluative.

[6]It is interesting to note that, when the first and third year residents were asked the first question, they produced a narrative-like summary of the operative procedure of a cholecystectomy in order of its performance. The fifth year residents generally produced more abbreviated commentary in answer to the first question, e.g., "Probably the critical things . . . we always explore the abdomen . . . you include what the gallbladder looks like . . ." A surgery professor's answer to the question "In cholecystectomies, which steps would be the most important for future reference?" was even more abbreviated: "Probably — well, none of them

Table 4.1.   Information Present in the Description of Procedure

Criteria	DrA 1	L*	DrJ 1	L*	DrR 1*	L*	DrS 1a*	1b*	L*	DrT 1	L
Type of incision	+	+	+	+	+	+	+	+	+	+	+
Layers of abdominal wall divided	+	+	+	−	+	+	+	+	+	+	+
Where abdomen entered	−	+	−	−	?	+	−	−	+	+	+
Cystic artery identification	+	?	+	+	+	+	−	−	+	+	−
Ease of finding cystic artery	−	−	?	−	−	+	−	−	+	−	−
Handling of cystic artery	+	+	+	+	+	+	+	−	+	+	+
Cystic duct identification	?	?	+	+	+	+	−	−	−	?	+
Ease of finding cystic duct	−	−	?	−	−	+	−	−	?	−	−
How cystic duct handled	+	+	+	+	+	+	+	+	+	+	+
Examination for stones in	−	+	−	+	?	+	+	+	+	+	−
Is common bile duct examined	−	?	−	+	+	+	+	+	+	+	−
Injury to common bile duct or not	−	−	−	−	−	−	−	−	−	−	−
If junction of duct could be identified	−	−	+	+	−	+	−	?	−	+	+
Cholangiogram done or not	−	+	−	+	+	+	+	+	+	−	−
If gallbladder taken from above or below	−	−	−	−	−	+	−	−	?	−	+
Suture material (of closing gallbladder bed?)	+	+	−	−	−	−	−	−	−	+	−
If gallbladder bed closed or not	+	+	−	−	−	−	−	−	−	+	−
If a drain put in	+	+	−	−	+	+	+	+	+	−	−

* = a cholangiogram and/or common bile duct exploration performed
+ = in the report
− = not in the report
? = some difficulty determining if information in the report or not

The answers to these questions yielded the information that is summarized in Tables 4.1 (Information Present in the Description of Procedure) and 4.2 (Information Present in the Description of Findings). In these tables, the first (1) and last (L) cholecystectomy report of each fifth year resident are also examined against the criteria.

Figure 4.1 shows schematically the differences in information recorded in the beginning and in the final reports, by resident. Note that, while information on both the procedure and findings increased, the larger increases are in the description of findings. We can also see from Figure 4.1

are terribly important, OK, but probably the most important would be any reference to the size of the bile duct or the size of the stones in the gallbladder, because these would have importance as far as if the patient later became jaundiced. Could the stones have moved from the gallbladder to the bile duct?"

Table 4.2.   Information Present in the Description of Findings

Criteria	DrA 1	DrA L*	DrJ 1	DrJ L*	DrR 1*	DrR L*	DrS 1a*	DrS 1b*	DrS L*	DrT 1	DrT L
Stones in gallbladder	−	+	−	−	+	−	−	−	+	−	−
Size of stones in gallbladder	−	+	−	−	+	−	−	−	+	−	−
Description of stones	−	+	−	−	+	+	−	+	+	?	−
Stones in duct	−	?	−	+	?	+	+	+	+	+	−
Size of common duct	−	?	−	+	−	+	−	−	+	−	−
Description of gallbladder	−	+	−	−	−	+	−	−	+	+	−
Infection of gallbladder	−	−	−	−	−	−	−	−	?	−	−
Thickened	−	−	−	−	−	−	−	−	+	−	−
Inflamed	−	−	−	−	−	−	−	−	+	−	−
Gangrenous	−	−	−	−	−	−	−	−	−	−	−
Normal	−	I	−	−	−	I	−	−	I	I	−
Distended	−	I	−	−	−	I	−	−	I	−	−
Small	−	+	−	−	−	+	−	−	−	−	−
Inflammation around gallbladder (including adhesions)	+	+	+	+	−	+	−	−	−	+	−
Exploration of abdomen	+	+	+	+	+	+	+	+	+	+	+
Small bowel	+	−	−	+	−	−	−	−	−	−	−
Kidney	+	+	+	−	−	−	−	−	+	+	+
Colon	+	+	−	+	−	−	−	−	+	+	+
Stomach	−	+	+	−	−	−	−	−	+	+	+
Hiatal hernia	−	−	−	−	−	+	−	−	+	−	−
Scarring of duodenum	−	−	−	−	−	−	−	−	−	I	−
Liver	+	−	+	+	−	−	−	−	+	+	+
Description of common bile duct	−	?	−	+	−	+	−	?	+	−	−
Indications for surgery	+	+	−	−	−	−	−	−	−	+	+
Bleeding or not	+	−	+	−	−	+	−	−	+	+	+

* = cholangiogram and/or common bile duct exploration performed
+ = in the report
− = not in the report
? = information may be in the report; difficult to interpret
I = informatmion interpretable based on other information in the report

that there are individual differences in the changes from the first report to the last report. Two residents, Dr. Rose and Dr. Shelton, made larger increases in both descriptions of procedure and findings than did the other residents. Dr. Shelton's increases are especially notable, since, in the "findings" portion of the beginning reports, very little information appears (two items in Text 1a, and three in Text 1b). In the final report, Dr. Shelton's descriptions of findings (DOF) not only increased dramatically (16 items, and two interpretable. By interpretable, I mean that some information can be assumed based on other information in the report; for example,

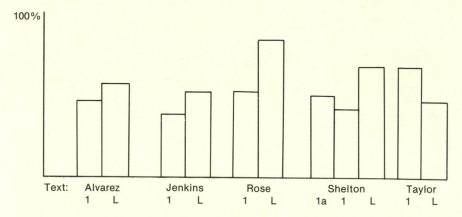

Percentage of Description of Procedure Information in First and Last Reports

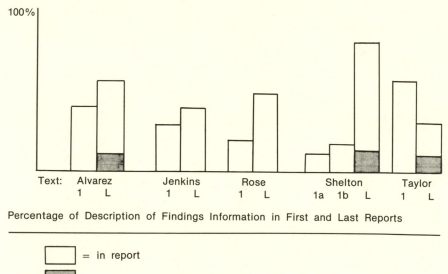

Percentage of Description of Findings Information in First and Last Reports

☐ = in report

▨ = inferrable information in report

Figure 4.1.   Differences in Information in First and Last Reports

the presence of a "small gallbladder" would presuppose that it is not distended), but also surpassed levels of information included by the other four residents. Dr. Alvarez's DOF increased also, but to a lesser extent than did Dr. Rose's and Dr. Shelton's. Dr. Jenkins showed little increase in reporting on the findings, and Dr. Taylor actually decreased the amount of information about both the procedure and findings in the first and last reports.[7]

Following a brief description of the residents and the data of the first and last operative reports analyzed, the rhetorical and linguistic manifestations of the differences between the first and last operative reports will be discussed.

The Fifth Year Residents

There are five fifth year residents in the surgical residency training program (names have been changed to protect confidentiality): four native speakers of English (Drs. Jenkins, Rose, Shelton, and Taylor), and one bilingual Spanish-English speaker (Dr. Alvarez). All the residents are male.

Because of some differences observed in the bilingual resident's reporting style, I was particularly interested in determining the role Spanish played in his medical education. I found that the role was not great. The bilingual resident received most of his education in the United States. He was born in the U.S. of Spanish speaking parents (his father and grandfather are also surgeons), lived in Puerto Rico until the age of 4 or 5, and then returned to the U.S. to live. He spoke Spanish at home as a child. His medical training was totally in English; he attended medical school in the U.S., except for a 2-month rotation in Puerto Rico, where all lectures and texts were in English. His use of Spanish in the medical context is confined to speaking Spanish with Spanish speaking patients and residents; he has never done medical records or other types of dictation in Spanish.

In-depth interviews (Paget 1983) were conducted with four of the five fifth year residents (Dr. Shelton was unavailable), as well as with a first and third year resident. The purpose of the interviews was to determine how the residents learned to dictate operative reports, as well as what information they considered important to include in cholecystectomy and gastrectomy operative reports.

Data

Reports of cholecystectomies dictated by all of these fifth year residents were collected from one of their five training sites. For the purposes of this

---

[7]It is not clear why there is a decrease in information from Dr. Taylor's first and last report. It may be that the procedure and condition reported on in Text L was less complex than that in Text 1, or it may be that conditions surrounding the reporting on the operation in Text L were such that less detail was reported; for example, the resident may have had to do several reports at the end of the day.

analysis, the reports of the first and the last cholecystectomy performed (see Table 4.3) (during the time of data collection) were chosen to be analyzed. In order that the first and last reports be as comparable as possible, the most routine uncomplicated reports were chosen, especially for the last reports. (Fifth year residents, since they are in their last year of training, generally have responsibility for more complex procedures than routine cholecystectomies.) In the case of one resident (Dr. Shelton), the absolute last case of a cholecystectomy that he dictated was not chosen to be analyzed, since that report was dictated 2 weeks following the operation. It was felt that the information in that report would not match the actual occurrences in the operation as closely as in a report that was dictated on the day of surgery. The report chosen to be included in the data base as Dr. Shelton's last report was dictated only 1 month prior to the above mentioned report; therefore, the amount of time between the two was not considered to be great. In selecting Dr. Shelton's first report to be analyzed, it was noted that he dictated two operative reports of cholecystectomies on one day; therefore, both reports are included in the data base.

It was not possible to find matched samples of reports which contained only the cholecystectomy procedure. That is to say, many cholecystectomies also include an x-ray procedure called a cholangiogram. This procedure is

Table 4.3.   First and Last Operative Reports Chosen for Analysis

Doctor	Length of training	Operative procedure performed*
Alvarez	6 months	Cholecystectomy
		Incidental appendectomy
Alvarez	4 years 8 months	Cholecystectomy
		Intracystic duct cholangiogram
Jenkins	1 year 6 months	Cholecystectomy
Jenkins	4 years 9 months	Cholecystectomy
		Intraoperative cholangiogram
Rose	4 months	Cholecystectomy
		Operative cholangiogram
Rose	4 years 1 month	Cholecystectomy
		Common bile duct exploration
		Intraoperative cholangiogram
Shelton-1a	2 months	Cholecystectomy
		Exploration of common bile duct
		Insertion of T-tube
Shelton-1b	2 months	Cholecystectomy
		Right breast biopsy
Shelton	4 years 5 months	Cholecystectomy
		(Intraoperative cholangiogram)
Taylor	8 months	Cholecystectomy
Taylor	4 years	Cholecystectomy

  * = Procedures are stated in same terminology as on operative reports
  ( ) = Procedure performed; not listed in identifying data in beginning of report

performed in order to show graphically the anatomy of the duct system and to detect any stones in the ducts (Dudley, Rob, and Smith 1977). Because this procedure is closely related to the cholecystectomy procedure, in some parts of the following analyses the information from the cholangiogram is included, and is so stated when it is included. The operative reports in the data base may also include additional operative procedures, such as an incidental appendectomy or a breast biopsy. In these cases, the additional procedure is not related to the cholecystectomy procedure proper, and so information from such procedures is not included in any analysis.

Rhetorical Differences between Description of Procedures and Description of Findings

At the beginning of this chapter, I focused on how residents included important information in their beginning and final reports. The preceding section does not, however, provide detail as to how information is structurally manifested in the texts. A linguistic analysis of the language of the texts, based on a rhetorical approach, will demonstrate the actual differences between the beginning and final texts. This discussion will focus, again, on the two language acts of describing procedures and describing findings, and ultimately on the manifestations of these acts in the data.

In describing a procedure that is to be followed, or that has been followed,[8] certain elements are typically involved: time or chronological succession, change, (Harris 1983), and instruments used to accomplish the procedure. We can see these elements in the following example, from a simple "how to" text, of instructions on how to prepare a tape for an answering machine:

1. Insert the Outgoing Message (OGM) Tape.
2. Turn the Volume Control to switch the power on.
3. Set the Function Selector to "OGM Rec."
4. Press the Start Button to reset the tape.

In this text, chronological succession is indicated through the numbering of the steps. Change of state can be inferred throughout the text, and the

---

[8]Most of the literature dealing with procedural discourse tends to focus on "how to" texts (cf. Harris 1983, Longacre 1976) as opposed to narrative descriptions of procedures that have already been completed. The discussion in this chapter recognizes that some similarities exist between operative reports and procedural discourse, with the exception that operative reports are narratives of completed procedures.

instruments (e.g., OGM tape, start button, etc.) are very salient and prominent parts of the text. Harris contrasts procedural discourse, which views the world as charge, with "purely descriptive discourse which knows the world spatially as stasis" (Harris 1983:141). It is important to note, as does Harris, that, in procedural discourse, varieties of complexities exist, from the above mentioned straight-forward step-by-step description of how a procedure should be done to more complex composites of process plus other rhetorical elements such as description, classification, evaluation and/or definition. Harris argues that, in the simplest texts, parts are put together in a sequence which corresponds to the temporal order in which activities are performed in the task. In more complex texts which may include additional rhetorical elements, however, parts are ordered by pragmatic principles that take into account users of the texts' needs.

Operative reports are similar to the above mentioned texts by virtue of the fact that their referent is a procedure. They differ from the above texts, however, because they have the additional narrative element (Labov and Waletzky 1967) of describing past events. As with the more complex composites of process plus other rhetorical elements described above, an operative report is both a narrative of a procedure that was followed and a description. There are descriptions of anatomical observations at certain key points in the narrative sequence. For example, after the surgeon makes an incision and enters the abdominal cavity (E3), he or she describes what he or she observes there (E4: exploration of the abdominal cavity.)

I argue here that the beginning texts tend to be a step-by-step description of a procedure with a greater focus on procedural elements in the text. In these beginning texts, we see more elements to indicate the chronological succession of the steps in the procedure. Markers of transition, such as temporal adverbs and certain types of adverbial clauses, are both more frequent and varied in these texts. For example, there are 65 markers of transition in the six beginning reports (average = 10.8) and 32 in the five final reports (average = 6.4). More mention of instruments used to accomplish the procedure are also observed--67 in the beginning reports (average = 11.1) and 27 in the final reports (average = 5.4). As a result, the procedural elements of these beginning texts appear to be "strung out". In addition, if we examine those parts of the operative reports which are prototypically procedural (such as E10: suturing the abdomen) as opposed to those parts which are prototypically descriptive (such as E4: exploration of the abdomen), more "narrative space" is taken to describe the former rather than the latter in the beginning reports. Interestingly, as I had observed in previous research with a NNS of English (NS of Spanish) (Pettinari 1985), the bilingual resident uses a particular sentence structure to mark transitions from one episode to another.

By contrast, the final texts are "something other" than a description of the procedure. Elements of the procedure are chunked into briefer portions of words, and phrases and more descriptive elements are observed, although the differences are not as dramatic as the above mentioned narrative transitions or instruments. For example, at the point in the procedure where an anatomic structure (especially one mentioned in the criteria) is encountered, it tends to be described. As a result, more descriptive elements are observed, such as what I term "creative" complex noun phrases (i.e., those which describe anatomical features of the patient, as opposed to complex NPs describing suture and instrument types). Complex noun phrases which incorporate observations of the agent (i.e., the surgeon) in the description (e.g., a *markedly* contracted gallbladder) are also observed. In contrast to the beginning texts, the prototypically procedural section of text (E10: suturing the abdomen) takes up less narrative space, although about as much detail in terms of anatomic structures is displayed in these final texts as in the beginning texts. Finally, a phenomenon which I term "telegraphic reporting" is found to a somewhat greater extent in the final reports than in the beginning reports. In telegraphic reporting, sentence elements such as the auxiliary *was, there,* or *we* appear to be "deleted," with a resulting bunching together of descriptive phrases, as in "Both ovaries within normal size and texture, a small retroverted uterus and a bladder semifull of urine."

Linguistic Reflections of Rhetorical Differences in the Beginning and Final Reports

In this section, I describe in detail the differences observed in both structure and content between the beginning and last texts. I present the remainder of this discussion in two parts: observations of features of the beginning texts, and observations of features of the final texts. As it is useful to contrast the two as I am discussing them, in many instances I present examples of beginning and final texts together. It is also important to point out here that, while there are differences between the beginning and final texts, as I have mentioned before, the differences are not absolute. Elements found in beginning texts may be found in the final texts, and vice versa. The difference is that the beginning and final texts tend to be weighted towards the following elements:

In TEXT 1:

1. There are more markers of transitions and more different types of transitional markers.
2. There is more mention of instruments.

3. More "narrative space" is taken to describe a prototypical procedural episode (suturing the abdomen) than to describe a prototypical descriptive episode (exploration of the abdomen).
4. *We* is a marker of transitions in the bilingual's reports.

TEXT L

1. There are more descriptive phrases scattered throughout the text.
2. There are more "creative" complex NPs.
3. There are more agent incorporating NPs.
4. There is more telegraphic reporting.

Text 1: There are More Markers of Transitions and More Different Types of Transitions

The narrative quality of operative reports is present in both the beginning and final reports. In both texts, the temporal sequence in the text apparently has some parallel with the temporal sequence (Labov and Waltezky 1967) of the surgical event, or, in any event, the order of episodes in all texts examined is quite similar. In the beginning reports, however, the temporal sequence of events is emphasized. One of the ways in which this occurs is that transitions from one event to another are marked lexically through temporal adverbs or phrases indicating movement from one event in time to another.

Recall that, in the text analyzed in the previous chapter (dictated by a first year resident; his first cholecystectomy), the temporal adverbs *next* and *then* and their textual functions were described. This report was typical of a beginning report. In that report, a number of instances of *next* and *then* were observed, and they appeared to perform functions in the text, such as listing, and switch reference. As we will see, the above quality and function of transition markers are typical of the beginning reports, but not of the final reports. Consider the contrasts between one part (E6: isolating the cystic artery) of the beginning and final reports dictated by two residents, Drs. Jenkins and Shelton:

(3) *Text 1*. Dr. Jenkins. E6.

Then using both blunt and sharp dissection using the Metzanbaum (sic)
      scissors and right angle clamps,
first the cystic artery was identified.
This was dissected free of surrounding tissues and using a right angle clamp,
a #2-0 silk tie was passed circumferentially.
This was tied
and *then* the two hemoclips were placed towards the gallbladder.

The artery was *then* divided between the two clips.

(4) *Text L*. Dr. Jenkins. E6.

The cystic artery was identified and divided between Hemiclips (sic).

(5) *Text 1b*. Dr. Shelton. E6.

The cystic artery was *then* isolated
    using blunt dissection with a right angle
    forceps.
This was *then* clamped
    using clips,
    two on the retained side of the artery
    and one on the gallbladder side of the cystic
    artery.
The cystic artery was *then* divided
    using Metzenbaum scissors.

(6) *Text L*. Dr. Shelton. E6.

. . . and the cystic artery was identified and ligated
    with 3-0 silk sutures and divided.

It is clear here that there are more temporal adverbs in the beginning texts than in the final ones. In addition, considerably more detail is included. In terms of the criteria of information considered to be important to include in this section of the reports, however, there is not a great deal of difference between the way in which the beginning and final reports match the criteria. Criteria for information to be included in E6 include "identification of the cystic artery, ease of finding the cystic artery, and how the cystic artery was handled." Dr. Jenkins's Texts 1 and L both include identification of the cystic artery and how the cystic artery was handled. Although Dr. Shelton's Text 1 includes considerable detail about how the cystic artery was isolated, clamped, and divided, it does not say specifically that it was identified: one of the criteria. Both Dr. Shelton's texts include information on how the cystic artery was handled.

It is clear in the above examples that what, in the first texts, is told in a narrative-like fashion is consolidated into one sentence in the final reports. It is also obvious that there are considerably more temporal adverbs in the first reports than in the final reports here. In addition, there is considerably more detail in the beginning reports as well. In both (3) and (5), more detail is given about the type of instruments used to accomplish the procedure, as well as the manner in which it is accomplished (e.g., "using blunt and sharp dissection"). Detail regarding areas adjacent to the procedure of tying the cystic artery (e.g., "this was dissected free of surrounding tissues") is included as well.

In consequence, we see more detail regarding specifics of the procedure in these beginning texts, and we also can observe other features of narrative organization that allow for the continuity of the topic through the narrative (Givon 1983), such as the use of pronouns.

Through all the detail in the beginning texts we can see clearer picture of the mechanics of the surgery as might be of interest to a beginner. As we read these sections of the procedure, the step-by-step nature of the surgery and the instruments used to perform that surgery are quite salient. Transitional devices such as temporal adverbs are one way in which the beginning resident continues the narrative.

If we examine the final texts dictated by all residents, there is a decrease in both the number of transitions and the types of lexical items which function as transitions (Table 4.4). All residents (with the exception of Dr. Rose, who only uses *then* as a transition marker) use fewer types of lexical items to mark temporal sequence. Note, in particular, that *first* is no longer used as a transition marker in any of the final reports. Thus, dividing a procedure into a number of discrete steps, beginning with step one, is no longer a way of reporting on the operation. As with the chess master, the more accomplished surgeon may no longer conceptualize the operation (for reporting purposes) in terms of separate entities.

Text 1: There is More Mention of Instruments

One feature commonly found in procedural texts is an indication of the instruments used to carry out the procedure. Operative reports share with procedural texts the feature of "telling how something is done or how something is made" (Longacre 1976:200). In telling how something is done, the instrument used to carry out the procedure is frequently an important element of that procedure. As already observed in examples discussed, instruments are a part of both the beginning and final texts. However, I now demonstrate that there is a decrease in the number of instruments mentioned from the beginning to the final texts. As an example, note the differences in the mention of instruments in Episode 3 (making the incision and entering the abdomen) in Dr. Shelton's beginning and final reports:

(7) Dr. Shelton - Text 1b - Episode 3

> A right subcostal incision was made over the existing right subcostal scar. Subcutaneous tissue was divided down using a *clean scalpel* and the anterior rectus sheath divided.

Table 4.4.   Number and Types of Transitions in Beginning and Final Texts

Text 1		Text L
Dr. A	4 *we then proceeded* (3EB) 2 *once* + past participle (1EB) participle 2 *then* (at end of episodes) 1 *we then* + verb (1EB) 1 *we also* + verb 1 *first* (=EB)	3 *once accomplished* (3EB) 1 *once in*
	11 TOTAL (6EB)	4 TOTAL (3EB)
Dr. J	10 *then* (3EB) 2 *after* + noun (2EB) 1 *first*	3 *then* (1EB) 2 *after* + noun (1EB) 1 *upon completion* (1EB)
	13 TOTAL (5EB)	6 TOTAL (3EB)
Dr. R	14 *then* (8EB)	8 *then* (6EB) 2 *after* + clause (1EB)
	14 TOTAL (8EB)	10 TOTAL (6EB)
Dr. S (1a)	2 *then* (2EB) 1 *it should also be noted (1EB)* 1 *after* + noun (1EB)	1 *after* + clause
	4 TOTAL (4 EB)	1 TOTAL
(1b)	8 *then* (8EB) 2 *after* + clause (2EB) 1 *upon* + gerund (1EB)	
	11 TOTAL (11EB)	
Dr. T	6 *then* (2EB) 3 *after* + clause or noun (3EB) 1 *attention was then turned* (1EB) 1 *upon* + gerund (1EB) 1 *at this point* (1EB)	10 *then* (4EB) 1 *upon* + gerund (1EB)
	12 TOTAL (8EB)	11 TOTAL (5EB)

(EB) = located at episode boundary

> The right rectus muscle was divided over an *Army-Navy retractor*
> and bleeding controlled using the *Bovie.*
> Posterior rectus sheath was grasped using *forceps*
> and the posterior rectus sheath and peritoneum entered.
> The posterior rectus sheath and peritoneum were divided using
> *Metzenbaum scissors.*

(8) Dr. Shelton - Text L - Episode 3

> A right subcostal incision was made two fingerbreadths below the costal
> angle from the midline laterally for approximately 15 cms.

Table 4.5. Mention of Instruments, Clamps, and Drains in Beginning and Final Texts

		Text 1	Text L
Dr. Alvarez		4	2
Dr. Jenkins		14	3
Dr. Rose		7	9
Dr. Shelton	(1a)	13	5
	(1b)	15	
Dr. Taylor		14	8
	Total	67	27

The subq. (sic) was divided.
The anterior rectus sheath was divided,
the rectus muscle divided
and hemostasis achieved with the *Bovie*.
The posterior rectus sheath, transversalis muscle and peritoneum entered
in the usual fashion.

One probable reason that the instruments are not mentioned as frequently in the final texts is that the resident assumes that the instruments are known to the skilled surgeon/user of the text. As a result the instruments need not be included in the report.

Another difference between the mention of instruments in the beginning and final reports again may relate to the focus on describing the procedure in Text 1 as opposed to the reduced focus (or chunking) of the procedure description in Text L. As additional evidence, we can see the reduction in the verb forms in this example (8) also. In the beginning text (7), for example, the separate maneuvers are expressed in a greater variety of verb forms: *divided down, divided, grasped,* and *entered*. In Text L (8), we see only two verbs used to describe the procedure: *divided* and *entered*.

The difference between the mention of instruments in the beginning and final reports (see Table 4.5) is rather dramatic; in all but one resident's (Dr. Rose) reports, there was at least a 50% decrease in the mention of instruments in the final texts.

Text 1: More "Narrative Space" is Taken to Describe a Prototypical Procedural Episode than to Describe Prototypical Descriptive Episode

As previously mentioned in this chapter, the exploration of the abdomen was an important piece of information to include. In developing the criteria, no residents mentioned suturing the abdomen as important information. Exploring the abdomen can be considered as a part of the operation

Table 4.6. Number of Words Used to Describe Two Sections of the Operative Report: Exploration of Abdomen and Suturing of Abdomen

	DESCRIPTION: Exploration		PROCEDURE: Suturing	
	Text 1	Text L	Text 1	Text L
Dr. Alvarez	75	64	108	71
Dr. Jenkins	47	100	52	63
Dr. Rose	22	32	86	42
Dr. Shelton	28/25	91	96/46	81
Dr. Taylor	127	117	61	33

that is "pure description;" in other words, the surgeon needs to observe the condition of the various organs in this section of the report, but no particular procedure is carried out in this part of the operation. Suturing the abdomen, on the other hand, can be considered to be"pure procedure." That is, when the surgeon manipulates the layers of abdominal wall to be sutured together, it would be unusual to find descriptive observations made about their condition.

Narrative space here simply means the number of words used to describe these parts of the reports. We can see from Table 4.6 that, despite the importance given to exploring the abdomen in the criteria, four of the five residents' Texts 1 use *more* narrative space to describe the prototypical procedure (PP), suturing the abdomen, than to describe the prototypical description (PD), exploring the abdomen. In their final texts, three of the five residents use *less* narrative space to describe the PP than the PD. Of those who continue to use more space to describe the PP than the PD, the difference is not great: nine more words for Dr. Alvarez, 10 more for Dr. Rose.

Although the number of words used can give us some hint of the relative importance of a part of the narrative, more helpful is the actual content of the passage. Here again, the principle of the change from a procedural text to a descriptive text holds (See Table 4.7). For example, in the prototypical

Table 4.7. Number of Words and Anatomic Structures in Describing Exploration of the Abdomen in Beginning and Final Texts

	Words		Anatomic Structures	
	Text 1	Text L	Text 1	Text L
Dr. Alvarez	75	64	8	10
Dr. Jenkins	47	100	3	6
Dr. Rose	22	32	0	0
Dr. Shelton (1a)	28	91	0	9
Shelton (1b)	25		1	
Dr. Taylor	127	117	11	16

description, exploring the abdomen, all but one resident mentioned *more* anatomic structures (and/or organs) in their final reports than in the beginning reports, whether or not they used more or fewer words (See Table 4.8). Two residents' PDs (Drs. Jenkins and Shelton) increased in length from Text 1 to Text L and also mentioned more anatomic structures. Two residents' PDs (Drs. Alvarez and Taylor) actually *decreased* in length from Text 1 to Text L, but they, too, mentioned more anatomic structures. One resident's PD (Dr. Rose) increased in length, but no anatomic structures were mentioned specifically in either the beginning or final texts.

If we examine the prototypical procedure, suturing the abdomen (see Table 4.8), we can see rather graphically the chunking of information relative to the anatomic description into less narrative space. Although less narrative space is taken by almost all residents in the final reports here, about as many anatomic structures are mentioned. No doubt part of the reason for this is that there are only so many layers of tissue that can be sutured together.

Let us examine how these differences between narrative space in the beginning and final reports and in the content of the information is expressed in excerpts from Dr. Shelton's reports. (Recall that Dr. Shelton was the resident whose reports increased the most according to the criteria.) Dr. Shelton's beginning report used 28 words to describe the exploration of the abdomen; his final report used 91 words. No anatomic structures were mentioned in describing the exploration of the abdomen in the first report; nine were in the final report. Suturing the abdomen used 96 words in the beginning report, 81 in the final; seven anatomic structures were mentioned in the first, and six in the final.

(9) *Text 1*. E4. Dr. Shelton. (28 words)

It should also be noted,
that at the beginning
of the operation,

Table 4.8.   Number of Words and Anatomic Structures in Suturing the Abdomen in Beginning and Final Texts

	Words		Anatomic Structures	
	Text 1	Text L	Text 1	Text L
Dr. Alvarez	108	71	5	5
Dr. Jenkins	52	63	5	8
Dr. Rose	86	42	3	3
Dr. Shelton (1a)	96	81	7	6
Shelton (1b)	46			
Dr. Taylor	61	33	5	4

after entering the peritoneum,
the entire abdominal cavity was explored,
and was found to be normal.

(10) *Text L.* E4. Dr. Shelton. (91 words)

The abdomen was explored.
The stomach was normal.
The hiatus was normal in diameter
    with no evidence
    of hiatal hernia.
The spleen was enlarged
    though normal consistency.
The left lower pole
    of the kidney was difficult
    to palpate.
The ascending transverse (sic), descending and
    sigmoid and rectum
    of the colon was all normal.
The liver was smooth and normal
    in size and consistency.
No masses were appreciated
    in the liver.
The gallbladder was somewhat thickened, showing
    signs of chronic cholecystitis
    with a single 2 cms.
    in diameter stone palpable
    in the fundus.

While both (9) and (10) both appear to describe more or less "normal" conditions in the abdomen (excepting the gallbladder in (10), in the last report the organs are named and their conditions given. Significant negative findings (for example, "the stomach was normal") are given, and the surgeon's judgments, based on technical expertise, are incorporated into this part of the text ("The left lower pole of the kidney was *difficult to palpate*," "No masses were *appreciated* in the liver"). In the final report, the gallbladder is described in detail, whereas there is no description of the gallbladder (in any part) in Text 1.

In Text 1, the organs are not named; the "entire abdominal cavity" is described as "normal." In fact, the greater portion (16 out of 28 words) of the narrative space is taken up in working out the mechanics of the temporal nature of the narrative itself. In Text 1, the description of the exploration is found out of sequence; rather than being the fourth episode, as is typical of the other reports analyzed, the exploration is mentioned later on in the text. This section, therefore, contains clauses to place the exploration in its proper place in the narrative sequence.

Suturing the abdomen, on the other hand, becomes a more compactly described section in the final report:

(11) *Text 1.* E10. Dr. Shelton. (96 words)

> After irrigation with copious amounts of normal
> saline, the peritoneum and the posterior rectus sheath
> was (sic) closed
> using #0-chromic, continuous suture.
> The anterior rectus sheath and transversalis muscle and
> fascia were then closed
> using #2-0 non-absorbable suture in figure of 8,
> and simple sutures.
> Subcutaneous tissue was not approximated
> although the subcutaneous tissue was irrigated
> with normal saline.
> The skin was closed
> using staples.
> A dressing was applied to the Penrose and the T-tube.
> The T-tube bag was placed on the T-tube,
> and the skin incision was washed
> and dried, and no dressing was applied.

(12) *Text L.* E10. Dr. Shelton. (81 words)

> The abdomen was irrigated with a liter of normal
> saline which contained one gm. of Kefzol.
> The patient was given one gm. of Kefzol at the
> beginning of the case by IV piggyback.
> No Penrose drain was placed.
> The posterior rectus sheath and peritoneum were
> approximated using a running O Vicryl suture
> and the linea alba and anterior rectus sheath were
> approximated with interrupted O Vicryl
> sutures.
> The subcu. (sic) was irrigated with antibiotic solution
> and the skin approximated with skin stapler.

In the first text, we can see markers of narrative sequence such as a dependent adverbial clause ("*After* irrigation with copious amounts of normal saline") and a temporal adverb (*then*). In the last text, although there is a reference to an earlier part of the operation ("The patient was given one gm. of Kefzol at the beginning of the case . . ."), it is not marked by any particular linguistic means. As in segments of these same texts by Dr. Shelton ((7) and (8), for example), there is a greater variety of verbs expressing similar acts in the first text ("closed" and "approximated") than in the last text ("approximated") only.

Other differences between (11) and (12) deal primarily with the extent of detail of the content. For example, the amount of saline administered is described as "copious" in the first text, but is more specifically described as "a liter" in the last text. Detail of the way in which the suture was tied ("figure of 8") and the washing and drying of the skin is not found in the last text.

Text 1: *We* Functions as a Marker of Transition in the Bilingual's Reports

A linguistic feature of the beginning texts, *we*, will be discussed briefly here because of its function in the discourse as a marker of transition, although it is found in only two residents' texts.[9] I show briefly in this section that, as in previous research (Pettinari 1985) which examined similar reports by a nonnative speaker of English who spoke Spanish as his first language, the *we* sentences function to mark transitions from one episode to another[10] or to mark transitions in subepisodes. What is interesting to me is that, in the bilingual's beginning reports, we see yet again a type of linguistic device to ensure the narrative flow of the text and to mark transitions from one episode to another. This linguistic device appears to be peculiar to those with a Spanish speaking background. *We* sentences are also interesting because they result in a different information structure (Brown and Yule 1983) in the beginning reports. I also briefly discuss this difference in information structure. As with the NNS reported on in Pettinari (1985), this resident decreases the use of *we* over time.[11]

Let us first examine Dr. Alvarez's reports to see how the five *we* sentences appear to mark transitions from one episode or subepisode to the next. *We* sentences are found to precede two episodes (E5: isolating the gallbladder, and E7: isolating and tying the cystic duct):

(Episode 5) *We then proceeded* to expose the gallbladder releasing the adhesions from the duodenum and the greater omentum, going down to the peritoneal area just over the cystic duct adjacent to the common duct.

(Episode 7) *We then proceeded* to expose the cystic duct with blunt dissection.

---

[9]Two instances of *we* are found in Dr. Taylor's beginning report, however. They do not function as a transition marker, though, and so will not be further discussed.

[10]These transitions were termed "change in focus of attention" in Pettinari (1985). In that study, I had not worked out determining episodes either.

[11]*We* is found in other reports dictated by this resident around the same time as the final report analyzed in this chapter. It is not found with as much frequency, however.

Three *we* sentences are seen without an episode (E10: closing the abdomen) also. What we see in Dr. Alvarez's Episode 10 is similar to that in the text examined in Chapter 3. Recall that, in Chapter 3, the beginning resident remarked that there were a number of substeps in Episode 10. In Dr. Alvarez's first text, not only does E10 appear to consist of a number of subepisodes, but, even more striking, the markers of transition are found in places similar to those in the Chapter 3 text:

(13) Dr. Alvarez: Text 1. E10 (--- = subepisode boundary that corresponds with that in (9)

> *We then irrigated* the abdomen with normal saline
> and checked to make sure
> that there was no bleeding in both operative sites.
> ---------------------
> Meticulous hemostasis had been obtained.
> ---------------------
> *We then proceeded* to close the peritoneum
> with 2-0 cotton interrupted sutures.
> ?------------------
> A drain had been placed at the cholecystectomy bed site
> and brought out through the base of the bottom of the wound.
> ---------------------
> *We also closed* the external rectus sheath
> with 2-0 cotton.
> Closed the subcutaneous tissues, Scarpa's fascia
> with 3-0 plain.
> Put staples into the skin
> and a 4-0 nylon stitch was placed to hold the drain
> in place at the base of the wound.
> Dry dressing was applied.

(14) Dr. Dobbs: Text 1, E10 (— = subepisode boundary notes by the resident)

> The abdominal cavity was *then* irrigated
> using normal saline.
> ---------------------
> Hemostasis was obtained
> ---------------------
> and the abdominal wall was closed.
> *First* the posterior rectus sheath was closed
> using 2-0 vicryl suture
> ---------------------
> *then* the anterior rectus sheath was closed
> using 2-0 vicryl suture
> ---------------------

The subcutaneous tissue was closed
   using 3-0 vicryl
and the skin was closed using staples.

Note the transitional markers before the subepisode of irrigating the abdominal cavity in both texts, and also before the following two subepisodes: closing the posterior and anterior rectus sheath in (14), and closing the peritoneum and external rectus sheath in (13). No transitional markers are found before hemostasis in either text.

Contrast the same episode in Dr. Alvarez's last text with his first, to see that there are no markers of transition:

(15) Dr. Alvarez: Text L, E10

   Once accomplished the area is irrigated.
   All packs removed
   and the posterior layer of abdominal wall closed
      with a running vicryl
   and the anterior layer of rectus sheath and external
      oblique closed with an interrupted 0 vicryl suture.
   The subcutaneous tissue was closed
      with interrupted 3-0 plain
   and the skin was closed
      with a running subcuticular 4-0 vicryl.
   Steri strips and dry dressings were applied.
   There were no drains left.

In Text L, there are no markers of transition, and the sentence level information structure has changed as well. What in Text 1 was "We then irrigated the abdomen with normal saline" has become "the area is irrigated" in Text L. Two-part verbs such as "proceeded to close" have changed to the passive "was closed." In places in Text L, telegraphic reporting is also seen; the auxiliary *was* is not present either, as in "and the posterior layer of abdominal wall closed with a running 0 vicryl." (There is a further discussion of telegraphic reporting later in this chapter.) In terms of the information structure of the message,[12] note that the various bits of information are located in different parts of the sentences in each of the following:

(16) We then proceeded to close the peritoneum with 2-0
   cotton interrupted sutures (A-Text 1)

---

[12]For a more complete discussion of information structure, see Brown and Yule (1983).

(17) . . . and the posterior layer of abdominal wall
closed with a running 0 vicryl (A-Text L)

In case grammar terms (Fillmore 1968), the information can be represented schematically as:

(16) agent-*then*-Vb-Vb-object-instrument
(17) object-vb-instrument

In the first text, information such as the agent, transitional marker, and two parts of the action — "to proceed" and "to close" — precede the structure being manipulated. In the last text, the structure being manipulated comes first in the sentence, the action follows, and then finally the instrument. In the final text, at least three bits of information are not present in the sentence: the actor, transitional marker, and one part of the action. As a result, the resident's focus, in the final report, has turned from the mention of surgeons and maintaining the sequence of the narrative, to the anatomic area affected and the surgical interventions made there.

On a larger textual plane, then (and I am not necessarily implying here that the sentence level organization precedes the textual organization, or vice versa), we see that the agent and actions come first in many of this resident's sentences in the beginning report. Contrast (13) with (15). Note, for example, the first bits of information in each texts. In (13), they are, in general, actions: "we then irrigated," "and checked to make sure," "we then proceeded," "we also closed," "closed the subcutaneous tissues," "put staples into the skin." In (15), they are entities — either anatomic features of the patient or significant negative findings: "the area is irrigated," "all packs removed," "the posterior layer of abdominal wall closed," "the anterior layer of rectus sheath and external oblique closed," "the subcutaneous tissue was closed," "and the skin was closed." Once again, we see another demonstration of the switch from focus on the procedure to focus on description.

In the preceding sections, I have shown that, in their beginning reports, residents focus on narrative elements of describing a procedure. This narrative of a procedure results in linguistic and lexical features which function to move the narrative along. Features such as markers of transitions and the use of *we* (in the bilingual's reports) function to ensure the temporal character of the narrative. The instruments used to carry out the procedure provide another focus of the beginning residents' reports. More narrative space is used to describe procedures than descriptive sections of the beginning reports. As a result of the above, the step-by-step nature of the surgery is a prime focus of attention of the beginning resident.

I now turn the focus of discussion towards the final reports. In particular, I discuss the descriptive nature of these texts. As previously illustrated, the procedural sections of the final texts are chunked into more consolidated sections, and I now show how parts of the patients' anatomy are described to a greater extent in the final texts. It should be noted that the descriptive differences between final and beginning reports that I am about to describe are not as great as in the previous sections discussed.

Text L: There are More Descriptive Phrases Scattered Throughout the Text

Recall that the criteria included descriptions of various anatomical features of the patient. These anatomical features included organs examined in exploring the abdominal cavity, as well as other anatomical areas encountered during the conduct of the operation. For example, according to the criteria, the gallbladder, the common bile duct, and stones in the gallbladder or the ducts should be described. Because of the narrative character of this genre, these descriptions of anatomic features that are not encountered during the course of exploring the abdomen tend to be offered at the point that the surgeon notes their presence in the flow of the narrative. I term these phrases, which describe anatomical features which are located within the flow of the narrative, as "scattered descriptors."

Consider, for example, how Dr. Alvarez includes a description of the cystic duct (Episode 7/9: isolating and tying the cystic duct) in his final report, but not in his first report:

(18) Dr. Alvarez: Text 1. E7/9

We then proceeded to expose the cystic
    duct with blunt dissection
Once exposed
    a right angle clamp was used for clamping
and 2-0 cotton ties also used to tie the cystic duct.
Cystic duct and cystic artery were both tied doubly with 2-0 cotton.

(19) Dr. Alvarez: Text L. E7/9

With sharp dissection the gallbladder is brought up
    into the abdominal wound,
clamps are placed on it
and sharp and blunt dissection reveals *a thin small*
    cystic duct and a cystic artery.
. . . The cystic duct itself is encompased (sic)
    and tied off distally with 2-0 cotton

and proximally towards the common duct
and another cotton tie for retraction.

Rather than merely naming the cystic duct, as in the beginning report, the resident adds descriptive adjectives to describe its size and width. In a cholecystectomy, frequently an ancillary procedure, a cholangiogram is performed along with the cholecystectomy. Since the purpose of the procedure is to examine the ductal structures, we might expect more descriptive terms in reporting on this procedure. Note the difference between Dr. Rose's beginning and final texts:

(20) Dr. Rose: Text 1. Cholangiogram

An operative cholangiogram was then performed
using Renografin 60 as the contrast media.
Free flow into the duodenum was seen.

(21) Dr. Rose: Text L. Cholangiogram

Intraoperative cholangiograms were then performed.
*There was obvious filling of the ductal structures
and free flow into the duodenum.*
No stone could be seen.

In this case, the description in the final text is more elaborate than that in the beginning text; pertinent negative findings are included ("no stone could be seen"), and the observations of the surgeon ("obvious filling") are incorporated into the description as well.

Obviously, there are a number of linguistic means to realize the scattered descriptors: complex NPs, *there* sentences, and noun clauses. There is a *tendency* for residents to increase the use of scattered descriptors; the increase is not absolute. As can be seen Table 4.9, not all residents increase

Table 4.9.   Number of Scattered Descriptors in Beginning and Final Texts

	Text 1	Text L
Dr. Alvarez	1	3 (1 − chol)
Dr. Jenkins	0	2 (1 − chol)
Dr. Rose	1 (not in chol)	7 (2 − chol)
Dr. Shelton (1a)	5 (1 − expl CBD)	3 (3 − chol)
	(1 − chol)	
(1b)	2	
Dr. Taylor	1	1

expl CBD = exploration of the common bile duct
chol = cholangiogram

in the use of scattered descriptors, and their presence may depend on whether a cholangiogram or other exploratory procedure such as a common duct exploration was performed.

Nonetheless, combined with other pheneomena, scattered descriptors are one means to realize the descriptive character of the final reports.

Text L: There Are More "Creative" Complex Noun Phrases

A well-documented feature of scientific and technical English is the complexity of the noun phrase. Phrases with a noun plus a number of nominal and adjectival modifiers, such as "a shortened enterohepatic circulating time" (Lee 1983), abound in medical journal articles, as well as in other published scientific and technical journal articles. Recent research on complex NP structure in the English for Science and Technology literature dealing with medical texts (i.e., Dubois 1981, Bruce 1984) has been concerned with the relationship of pre- and postnominal modification of writers' assumptions about information shared with readers.

Although no discernable pattern could be observed in pre- and postnominal modification in these data, there is a pattern of increase in two types of complex NPs: what I term "creative complex NPs" and "agent incorporating NPs." I discuss these in this section and in the subsequent sections. For the purpose of this discussion, I define "complex NP" as a noun plus at least two nominal or adjectival modifiers, as in "normal caliber duct." (An anatomic structure consisting of more than one lexical item, e.g., cystic duct, is considered to be one "word.") Therefore, "cystic duct stump" would not be considered a complex NP. (Generally, NPs with prepositional phrases, such as "posterior layer of abdominal wall," are not considered either.)

A number of complex NPs can be found in both the beginning and final texts. A first examination of the reports reveals that phrases such as "4-0 nylon suture," "a #14 French T-Tube," and "a running 0-Vicryl suture" can be found in all texts, beginning and final. NPs such as these, which refer to suture and instrument types, are not unlike "unanalyzed units" (Hakuta 1974) described in the Second Language Acquisition literature. I choose to borrow this term since it appears that these phrases are somewhat "fixed;" like the second language learner, the beginning resident uses a complete phrase "borrowed" from the surrounding speaking community, but does not necessarily create complex NPs to describe novel observations of the patient's anatomy encountered.

In the beginning reports, then, fewer "creative" complex NPs are found. That is to say, fewer complex NPs describe novel phenomena observed in the patient during the course of the operation. Consider Table 4.10.

The list is brief and perhaps slightly unimpressive. Part of the problem,

Table 4.10.   Creative Complex NPs in Beginning and Final Texts

In Beginning Texts	
a small rock hard fibroid 1 by 1 cm. in size	(Alvarez)
rather large cystic duct stump	(Alvarez)
several bleeding points	(Jenkins)
rather large cystic duct stump	(Shelton)
In Final Texts	
normal kidneys bilaterally	(Alvarez)
normal pancreatic head and tail	"
a small retroverted uterus	"
a bladder semifull of urine	"
thin small cystic duct	"
normal sized ducts	"
single 2 cm. in diameter stone	(Shelton)
normal caliber duct	
no mass lesions	(Taylor)
a few small diverticula	

though, is that it is somewhat arbitrary to separate off the creative complex from the context of the complete noun phrase and to count only the NPs without prepositional phrases. As with all phenomena observed, there are some individual differences in how certain functions are realized linguistically. Dr. Jenkins, for example, produced a number of creative NPs involving prepositional phrases in the final reports. It is interesting to examine the NPs with prepositional phrases in both his beginning and final texts (see Table 4.11).

The NPs in the beginning report primarily denote locations of anatomic features, but the NPs with prepositional phrases generally denote descriptions of conditions. This provides yet another example of the observation that the final reports become a more descriptive document.

Text L: There Are More Agent Incorporating NPs

Another type of descriptive noun phrase found in these data are what I term "agent incorporating NPs." These are noun phrases that incorporate the physician's observations into an adjective such as "palpable," and there are more of these in the final reports. Adjectives such as "palpable," "visible," and "marked" imply that the surgeon "felt," "looked," and "noted" without expressing such actions in a verb phrase. Here, again, we see somewhat more agent incorporating NPs in the final reports than in the beginning (see Table 4.12):

Again, examining one of these agent incorporating NPs in its sentence or discourse context indicates more complexity in terms of the text in the hospital context. Agent Incorporating NPs appear to provide a means for

Table 4.11.   Noun Phrases with Prepositional Phrases in Dr. Jenkin's Texts

In the Beginning Report
induction of the general anesthesia
the gallbladder near the infundibulopelvic
peritoneum over the porta hepatis
junction between the cystic duct, commom hepatic, and common bile duct
the site of puncture
several bleeding points in the gallbladder bed
area of the gallbladder bed and operation

In the Final Report
induction of general endotracheal anesthesia
no mass in the area of the appendix or sigmoid colon
marked inflammatory reaction in the area of the gallbladder with adhesions of the transverse colon and duodenum
some areas of fat necrosis along the upper border of the head of the pancreas
some small amount of hematoma in the retroperitoneal tissues
junction between the common hepatic and common bile duct
free flow of contrast into the duodenum
area of the dissection
several points on the bed

Table 4.12.   Agent Incorporating NPs in Beginning and Final Texts

In the Beginning Reports
   single 2 cms. in diameter stone *palpable* in the fundus   (Alvarez)
   no *palpable* stone   (Taylor)

In the Final Reports
   non *visible* dilatation of the vessels   (Alvarez)
   marked inflammatory reaction   (Jenkins)
   visualized ducts   "
   easily *palpable* stone   (Rose)
   no *palpable* stones   (Shelton)

the surgeon to express his or her limitations in observing. In other words, the surgeon is recognizing that other phenomena may be there, but they were not phenomena that he or she could "see" or "feel." In the cholangiogram portion of one final report, for example, *visualized* takes on a more complicated meaning than "seen" or "observed." *Visualized* could be interpreted to indicate a hedging that restricts the exact location where an observation was made:

(22) Dr. Jenkins. Text L. Cholangiogram

   Two pictures were taken
   and both appeared normal
   although the left hepatic system was poorly seen no stones were

identified
within the *visualized* ducts
and there was free flow of contrast into the duodenum.

One interpretation of "visualized ducts" could be "those that we could see." In other words, the surgeons may have been unable to see the left hepatic system well; no stones were identified within those ducts that could be seen. In this case, the agent incorporating NP functions to express the limitation on the resident's ability to observe. A term such as "palpable" could also function this way. A sentence such as "there were no palpable stones in the gallbladder" could also be taken to mean that there might have been stones, but none that could be felt.

Text L: There is More Telegraphic Reporting

A phenomenon closely related to complex NPs and agent incorporating NPs is what I term "telegraphic reporting." In a phrase such as:

no stones *palpable* in the common bile duct

is *palpable* part of a complex NP describing "stones?" Is there a "deleted" auxiliary *were*, resulting in *palpable* as a predicate adjective? Rather than concern ourselves overly much about how to categorize such phenomena, a more interesting exercise would be to examine some examples of the discourse nature of telegraphic style, and the resulting density of text. Contrast Episode 4 (exploration of the abdominal cavity) in Dr. Alvarez's final report with his beginning report (verbs have been italicized).

(23) Dr. Alvarez. Text 1. E4.

Exploration of the abdomen *showed* a small rock hard fibroid 1 by 1 cm in size on the right part of the uterus.
The uterus *was* normal in size. The ovaries *were* normal.
No cul-de-sac or adnexal masses.
Colon and intestines *were* free of any masses.
The spleen *was* slightly enlarged but within normal limits.
Liver *was* smooth.
The gallbladder *was* adhesed and stuck to by duodenum.
The rest of the exploration and kidneys *were found* to be within normal limits.

(24) Dr. Alvarez. Text L. E4.

Once accomplished,

exploration of the abdomen *revealed* normal stomach and spleen, normal
   kidneys bilaterally, normal pancreatic head and tail, large intestine,
   ascending, traverse and descending, rectum normal.
Both ovaries within normal size and texture,
a small retroverted uterus and a bladder semifull of urine.
Non visable (sic) dilation of the vessels
and the gallbladder itself *had* some gravel within it.
It *is* small without adhesions.

The final report (24) results in a categorization of the phenomena
observed: (a) normal organs first, as a category, such as "exploration
reveals normal _____ ,_____ , . . ."; (b) particular organs commented
upon, i.e., "both ovaries within normal size and texture"; and (c) commentary upon the gallbladder. In terms of information quantity, the absence of
the auxiliary does not contribute to any loss of information.

The beginning report, in contrast, results in a section in which the
information does not appear to be categorized in any particular way.
Organs appear to be mentioned one by one. (For another example of change
to telegraphic reporting that this resident does, see (13) and (15).)

Telegraphic reporting is another of those individual reporting styles that,
if present in the resident's repertoire in the beginning reports, increases in
the final reports.

Conclusion

In this chapter, I have demonstrated that operative reports of a routine
operation, cholecystectomy, do change over the five-year period of these
residents' training. The change can be seen in both what is reported on and
in how that is expressed linguistically. I have argued that, in the beginning
reports, the procedural narrative "drives" the reporting of the surgery. In
very general terms, I have shown that, in a number of ways, the recounting
of the narrative of the operation is what happens in the beginning reports.
In effect, the resident is saying, "This is what I did." A number of features
of procedural narrative are present in that story: the sequential narative of
the narrative is expressed overtly, and the instruments used are included.
The fifth year resident, not unlike the chess master discussed in Hofstadter
(1979), produces a "higher level description" that summarizes in capsule
form the procedural sections of the narrative and amplifies the descriptive
sections of the report. In effect, this resident is stating, "This is what I
observed."

This finding is congruent with the few studies in text acquisition. Eiler
(1983) examines high school students' acquisition of the genre of literary

criticism, and notes a movement from recounting to interpretation. Martin (1983:37) examines the development of register in young children (or what I have been terming *genre*), and notes that children tend to "reweight the inherent possibilities in his/her linguistic potential with respect to context in a way that is considered appropriate in his/her culture."

In the next chapter, I suggest some medicolegal implications of the difference between the beginning and final reports and offer suggestions to restructure the narrative to make it more "reader-based prose."

CHAPTER 5

IMPLICATIONS OF THIS STUDY

This study examined routine "normal" cases that occur in the day-to-day operation of hospital business. The operation observed and described in Chapter 2 was, to my knowledge, not problematic. The patient recovered and went home to resume her normal life, according to the resident. The operative procedure reported on and examined in Chapters 3 and 4, cholecystectomy, is a fairly common operation. First and second year residents assist in these operations. In this study, my purpose has been to examine the reporting process and the acquisition of the genre. In order to do this, I have examined a relatively uncomplex type of operation.

Before discussing medicolegal implications of this study, I wish to emphasize that the data examined are not, to my knowledge, of particularly high risk situations. In no way am I suggesting that they are situations in which an established standard of care was not met. I am pointing out that in routine, uneventful situations, such as those examined in this study, loss of information from the operation to the reporting on the operation occurs. Chapter 2 reveals that features of the reporting process result in loss of information from the operation to the reporting on the operation. Gaps in information also are uncovered in the examination of the evolution of reporting styles described in Chapter 4. These gaps in information, while no doubt inadvertent (and it is likely that the surgeons and residents themselves are unaware of these gaps), could have had medicolegal consequences if the medical records had been subpoenaed.

In Chapter 1, a typology of audience interest in operative reports was given, based on a fifth year resident's observations of his experience. The first category of audience interest was "memorandum for file"; here, there would be little future interest in the case. In light of the legal implications of surgery, and in light of the need to produce a legally defensible account of the surgery, it would seem that, even if the report is a "memorandum for file" (as no doubt many of the operations reported on here are), information gaps be avoided to the greatest extent possible.

Information gaps are potentially serious, since, legally, the absence of entries on the medical record implies that nothing was done (Rozovsky 1978). These gaps can, in many cases, be avoided. In this section, I point out some gaps in information, and offer suggestions to remedy the situation.

A malpractice case can come to trial anywhere from 2 to 10 years after the event (Good Medical Records 1983). As a result, the medical record is usually the only documentation available to prove what happened and is, in fact, the most important evidence in a malpractice trial (Gregory 1982). Juries are more likely to believe documented evidence of the case than a witness who is relying on memory of an event that occurred several years ago (Rozovsky 1978). It stands to reason, then, that, if the medical record is well documented, it lessens the chance that a plaintiff can prevail in court (Squire 1985).

The surgical specialties are involved in litigation more frequently than the nonsurgical specialties (Zaslow 1978). In New York State, for example, the three specialties with the highest percentages of malpractice cases are neurosurgery, orthopedic surgery, and obstetrics/gynecology (Squire 1985). In consequence, the operative report is an extremely important piece of documentation, not only for medical purposes, but also for the surgeon's legal defense. It is in the surgeons' interest that this report be completed in the most accurate way possible. While a number of publications in the medical literature point out the importance of medical record reporting for the legal defense of the physician, and offer practical suggestions about how physicians and surgeons should record information (Matte 1971, Korcok 1977, Rosovsky 1978, Good Medical Records 1983, Kerr 1983), to my knowledge, the present study is unique in that it examines the surgical reporting process and pinpoints where information gaps may occur.

Chapter 2 examined and analyzed the relationship between the operating room talk and the dictation of the operative report. One section of the talk examined was the pathologist's call to the operating room on the results of the frozen section. The conversation was as follows:

Path: d'doctor_____ calling on the frozen
Dr: yeah
Path: ((names his full name)). A single cell neoplasm totally benign. Looks like either a neurolemoma or a leiomyoma
Dr.:   you think it's benign though, right?
Path: That's what it looks like, fine

The reporting on this section of the operation in the operative report (dictated by the resident) stated:

The frozen section on the mass in the stomach came back as a benign probable leiomyoma.

In the talk, the pathologist states "a single cell neoplasm totally benign," and hedges about the differential diagnosis of the tumor, "*looks like* either a neurolemoma or a leiomyoma." The surgeon's partial repeat of the pathologist's diagnosis, "you think it's benign though, right?" is a standard form of confirmation (Beckman and Frankel 1984). This partial repetition or paraphrase commonly functions to provide the first speaker the opportunity to repeat or clarify the information. Here, the information which is perhaps more immediately significant, that is, the fact that the tumor was benign, is clarified. The differential diagnosis is not.

In the operative report, the pathologist's exact words were not noted; "single cell neoplasm" and "neurolemoma" did not appear in the operative report. I might add here that, in transcribing the tape, I could not hear this section of the transcript with any clarity at all because of background noise. "Neurolemoma" was particularly difficult to hear. In playing the tape back with the surgeon and a resident, we needed to replay the tape a number of times to be able to determine the pathologist's exact words. Of course, regarding the operation itself, we no longer can determine if "neurolemoma" or "single cell neoplasm" were heard by either the surgeon or by the resident who dictated the operative report. It is possible that they were not heard, or it is possible that they were heard but were not recorded on the operative report.

The inability to hear and/or completely process spoken discourse in a complex, professional, highly stressed situation is not unique to surgeons, of course. Transcripts of airline pilots' conversation in aviation accidents (Goguen and Linde 1983), and of airline flight simulation (Frankel 1985), reveal that the communication dynamics between crew members can result in misinterpretations and misunderstandings. A multiplicity of conversational demands on the pilot in a three-way interaction between air traffic control, pilot, and copilot can be a source of difficulty (Frankel 1985).

In this segment of the operation, there is also a three-way communication situation, although it is unlikely that anyone present in the operation would have recognized it as such. From the medical point of view, the conversation between the pathologist and surgeon establishes the fact that the tumor was benign. From the reporting and medicolegal point of view, the resident, as the reporter of the operation, is also a part of the conversation, as an auditor. As there is no videotaped evidence of the activity of the surgery, it is not obvious what the resident was doing at the time of the pathologist's call. Yet he was the immediately responsible party for reporting on the operation. (The surgeon, of course, is ultimately responsible for authenticating the operative report, but the time lag between the operation and authenticating the operative report can be a number of days. Consequently, the surgeon may forget details of an operation, especially a routine one.)

In order to prevent the information gap that was observed here between the operation and its reporting, a speech act could be designed whereby the surgeon take into account the resident's role as reporter of the operation. Rather than a partial repeat of the pathologist's diagnosis for his own clarification purposes, the surgeon could repeat the entire differential diagnosis. This could enable the pathologist to both clarify the differential diagnosis, and could enable the resident to hear clearly what the differential diagnosis is for reporting purposes.

In Chapter 4, information gaps between the operation and the reporting on the operation are also observed, but of a different type. In Chapter 2, because the operation was observed and audiotaped, it is easier to trace the information gaps between operation and reporting with some precision. In Chapter 4, because the operations were not observed, we can only assume that the parts of the operation were present in the operation but were not reported on. The information gaps here may be attributable to the first year residents' lack of precise knowledge about information to be included in the operative report, or it may be due to individual differences in the detail included in a resident's reporting style. The information gaps may also be due to the narrative structure of the operative report.

Zaslow (1978) points out the importance of conducting a thorough exploration of the abdomen in cases where a diagnosis is uncertain. Two malpractice cases are cited where such an exploration was not conducted in order to determine the cause of symptoms. In addition, Stanley-Brown (1983:110) warns residents that, "if you are in the habit, and you should be, of exploring the abdomen completely, a careful description of all organs must be included."

In the data examined in Chapter 4, all beginning residents noted that the abdomen was explored. The extent of detail in the description varied, however.

Table 5.1 shows that three residents, Drs. Alvarez, Jenkins, and Thomas, named some of the organs and anatomic structures in both the beginning and final report. (The organs and anatomic structures are from the criteria of information important to include, given by the fifth year residents.) Out of seven structures, Dr. Alvarez named four in the beginning report and three in the final report; Dr. Jenkins named three in the beginning and three in the final report; and Dr. Thomas, five in the beginning and four in the final. One resident, Dr Sheldon, named no structures in the beginning reports, but did name five in the final report. One resident, Dr. Rose,

Table 5.1.   Description of Exploration of Abdomen in Beginning and Final Reports

	Dr.A.		Dr.J.		Dr.R.		Dr.S.			Dr.T.	
Small bowel	+	−	−	+	−	−	−	−	−	−	−
Kidney	+	+	+	−	−	−	−	−	+	+	+
Colon	+	+	−	+	−	−	−	−	+	+	+
Stomach	−	+	+	−	−	−	−	−	+	+	+
Hiatal hernia	−	−	−	−	−	+	−	−	+	−	−
Duodenal scarring	−	−	−	−	−	−	−	−	−	+	−
Liver	+	−	+	+	−	−	−	−	+	+	+

+ = in the report
− = not in the report

named no structures in the beginning and one in the final. It would appear here that including a description of all organs examined is an individual matter of choice (but observe the difference between Dr. Sheldon's beginning and final reports). It would also seem for future reference, from a medical and legal standpoint, that it would be incumbent to include all organs and anatomic structures.

Another descriptive item with potential medicolegal consequences on the cholecystectomy reports is the description of the common bile duct. Here, the differences between first and fifth year residents is more obvious. The medicolegal consequence of the lack of inclusion of this information can be serious, according to a textbook on medicolegal aspects of surgery (Ficarra 1968:268):

> Since stones are present in the common bile duct in 5 to 10 percent of patients with acute cholecystitis, exploration of the common bile duct should be performed when the indications therefore are present. If either choledochotomy or choledochostomy is not performed *a written notation on the patient's hospital record should be made indicating the reasons why exploration was not performed or could not be done.* (emphasis added)

In the data examined in this study, the following was noted (see Table 5.2):

Here, in the beginning reports, no residents described the common bile duct. In the final reports, three of the five did, along with one report in

Table 5.2.   Exploration of Common Bile Duct in Beginning and Final Reports

	Dr.A		Dr.J		Dr.R		Dr.S			Dr.T	
CBD description	−	?	−	+	−	+	−	?	+	−	−
Stones in duct	−	?	−	+	?	+	+	+	+	+	−

+ = in report
− = not in report
? = informatmion may be in the report; difficult to interpret

which it was unclear whether the common bile duct was described or not. Regarding stones in the duct, two beginning residents mentioned the presence or absence of stones in the duct; two did not, and one report was difficult to interpret. In the final reports, three mentioned the presence or absence of stones; one did not, and one final report was difficult to interpret.

The size of the data sample is small here, and so it is difficult to state with any certainty whether the reason for including or not including this information is due to the level of training or to individual differences. However, I would suggest that a hypothesis based on the narrative structure of these reports can be made which offers an explanation of why residents tend to include a more detailed description of the abdomen than of the common bile duct. In the narrative of the operation itself, the exploration of the abdomen is considered to be a separate episode, and a prototypically descriptive one. Beginning residents "have" this particular episode in their script of these reports. The description of the common bile duct, on the other hand, is not considered to be a separate episode. Rather, as the common bile duct is manipulated during the course of the operative procedure, it may or may not be described in the report. In a sense here, the strictly narrative structure of the "scripts" that residents (and surgeons) follow may well mitigate against the inclusion of descriptive elements in the procedural section of the narrative. This lack of differentiation between descriptive and procedural elements in describing the operation may occur particularly in the beginning of residency training, when the resident may not have clearly in mind the kinds of information that are needed for future reference.

One possible way to eliminate the burying of descriptive information in the procedural section of the narrative, and to make the inclusion of descriptive elements more salient to beginning residents, would be to redesign the "format" of these operative reports to encourage more reader-based prose. Flower (1981) points out that, rather than simply reciting information as it is stored in memory, reader-based prose takes into account the readers' needs for a different organization of information. Redesigning the format of these reports to account for readers' needs for information on the findings of the operation could result in the following type of text. Rather than having one long narrative description of the operation, with both descriptive and procedural elements, the report could be divided into two sections (as I observed at one hospital). The first section, *operative findings*, would describe in detail the condition of the structures observed and manipulated. The other section, *description of procedure*, would describe the actual performing of the procedure.

Besides changing the structure of the operative reports, a responsibility of hospital administration and appropriate committees, surgical residency training programs might also weight the risks and benefits of more formalized instruction in both operative report dictation and also in other types of medical record reporting. For example, to my knowledge, no criteria for information to include in operative reports are available for beginning residents. It appears that learning to operate is a gradual on-the-job training process, with a great deal of supervision from faculty. Learning to report on operations is also a gradual on-the-job process, but with little or no formal supervision or training from faculty. The question remains whether hospitals can afford the resulting documentation.

It would seem important that this information be included for medicolegal purposes. Having reports where this information is not included may well be a luxury for both the hospital and for the surgeons involved.

CHAPTER 6

CONCLUSIONS

In an article titled "The High Cost of Low Frequency Events: the Anatomy and Economics of Surgical Mishaps" in the *New England Journal of Medicine,* Couch, Tilney, Raynor, and Moore (1981:637) point out that:

> Medical misadventure (i.e. difficulties resulting from error) blends into the dense matrix of high-technology medicine and is easily obscured by it.

By the same token, reporting in hospitals, as well as in other institutions no doubt, is also a dense matrix of processes which may well be obscured by the technologies involved in the reporting. Other factors obscuring the reporting processes include the number of contexts that produce the final written report.

This study has examined one type of reporting, reporting on operations, from a linguistic point of view, and has attempted to unravel the matrix within which these texts are created by examining the text from various points of view.

After discussing the relationship between the operative report and other texts on the medical record, I have examined the operative report as an institutional text from three perspectives. These perspectives include:

(1) The relationship between the operative report and the surgical event: the relationship between the talk in the operating room and the dictation of the report.

(2) The internal structure of the text: the relationship between prosodic and grammatical features and the episodic structure as perceived by the resident dictating the report.

(3) The change in reporting styles over time: the contrast between reports dictated in the first and last years of residency training.

This approach yields a rich source of interpretive explanation of both the text and of the context surrounding the text. Because of the complex matrix within which reporting occurs, an examination from only one point of view would provide a more incomplete view of the text. For example, if only (1), the relationship between the talk in the operating room and the operative report, was examined without (2), the internal structure of the text, it would be difficult to know which parts of the operative report corresponded to parts of the operation. If (1) had been examined without an understanding of (3), the change in reporting styles over time, we would not know that the complex NP that the resident uses to describe a tumor is more typical of an advanced resident than of a beginning resident.

An examination of (2), the internal structure of the text (in this case produce by a first year resident), even utilizing the insights of a specialist informant, would yield a skewed view of these texts without a contrast of reporting of the first and fifth year residents. The examination of (2) without the contrast in (3) might have led to the conclusion that lexical markers of narrative transition are an integral part of these texts. An examination of reports dictated by fifth year residents reveals that, for more experienced residents, this is not so. The examples could continue.

Reporting and documenting the care given to patients is done routinely in hospitals; it is an integral part of most ongoing activities in a hospital. For the purposes of medical communication (as opposed to bureaucratic record keeping), reporting and communicating between professionals can provide the principal purpose of a medical event, or recording can occur post hoc the event, or, in some cases, the relationship can comprise both the purpose and the follow-up of the event.

The operative report is one of the many texts created by professionals regarding the patient's condition and reaction to treatment. Some texts on the medical record are cotextual with the operative report; that is, the referent of the text is an aspect of the operation. Many of these texts are created by professionals other than the surgeon. For example, in an operation for carcinoma, both the operative report and the pathology report serve differing functions in the description of the patient's condition. Surgeons excise tissue and describe that tissue, but the definitive diagnosis is given by the pathologist. The surgeon, however, has access to the entire area examined within the operation, and it is only through his or her report that the extent of the disease in the patient can be noted.

I suggest that the communicative role of the operative report, in the further care of the patient and for its potential audience, depends upon the role of the surgical event in the illness of the patient. Three types of audiences were explored, along with contingencies that could change the interest that various groups might have in the operative report. The first audience type is *memorandum for file*. This audience is, in fact, little or no audience. Here, the operation is an event which terminates the condition that brought the patient to the operating room, and there is little future need for the report. An adversary audience may have interest in a report of an operation which creates a new chain of events resulting in negative life changes for the patient. Medical audiences are especially interested in the reports when the patient has a problem, such as carcinoma, which will require future care. In the event of contingencies, both medical and adversary audiences may have interest in these reports.

The study was concerned with examining the role of the learner in the "language game" (Wittgenstein 1958) of producing these textual records. This type of reporting is rarely formally taught, nor are the rhetorical acts of describing findings and describing procedures commonly formally presented. As a result, residents employ a number of self-teaching strategies to learn how to complete these reports. All residents expressed anxiety over doing these reports in the beginning of their training.

This study examined the relationship between the talk that occurs in an operation and the reporting on the operation. The language acts in the operation were classified according to a dramaturgical model (Goffman 1959). Some language acts are "backstage," i.e., for the purposes of the group. Humorous comments, instructing, and casual conversation are all examples of "backstage" talk which, while important for the solidarity of the group, are not of interest to potential audiences of these reports, and, therefore, do not get reported on in the reports. Some language acts are "mixed," such as planning and decision making, in that the results of the language acts are included in the reports, but the language acts themselves are not reported on. Other language acts, such as determining the diagnoses, are reported on, however. The report does not necessarily reveal the precise order of events as they unfold during the operation, nor does it reveal sociolinguistic features of talk, such as hedging and the collaboration that occurs among participants in the operation. The representation of the diagnosis increased in specificity during the temporal course of the operation, but this increase in specificity was not captured in the operative report examined in this study. As Cicourel (1975) notes, medical summaries are like a "folk practice" where stories are told in fairly standardized ways even though the original experience might not have occurred in quite this way.

In order to begin to contrast the reports dictated by beginning residents and by residents at the end of their residency training, the internal structure of one report of a cholecystectomy was examined in depth. The goal of the analysis in Chapter 3 was to determine the plot of the text, or the "set of constraints on the selecting and ordering of episodes or motifs" (Becker 1980:226). In order to do so, a methodology for analysis was devised which set up a series of observational points in the evolution of the "official" record. In contrast to many studies in discourse analysis, this methodology takes into account the transformation of texts from spoken to written, and the segmentation of the text is informed by the person who aided in its construction. As the resident who assisted in the operation was dictating this type of operative report for the first time, this in-depth study provided a useful baseline in the contrast between first and fifth year residents' reports, also.

In Chapter 3, it was pointed out that there are two macrolevels of structure in this text: (a) the formatting of certain information on the page of the report, and (b) the episodic structure of the narrative summary of the operation. The resident's spoken summary of the operation comprise the macropropositions of the episodes. The spoken, dictated text was examined for phonological and prosodic features; and the written, orthographic text was examined for the correspondence of those features with grammatical cues to narrative structure.

Episodes proved to be a useful heuristic for beginning to examine the longitudinal data in Chapter 4. Using episodes as a unit of analysis provided a useful tool to enter these texts. Information other than the structure of episodes were examined in the contrastive study, however. The content of information on these reports was examined also, and it was determined that the content changes over time. Criteria of information considered important to include were established through interviews with the fifth year residents. It was determined that, in general, residents increase in their reporting on information regarding the procedure, as well as on elements of the findings over the course of 5-year residency training period. The reporting on the findings increased to a somewhat greater extent, however.

Moreover, in the beginning texts, it is easy to see influence from the narrative genre. In these beginning texts, there are more markers of transitions as well as more different types of transitional markers. There is more mention of instruments. More "narrative space" is taken to describe a prototypical procedural episode, suturing the abdomen, than to describe a prototypical descriptive episode, exploration of the abdomen.

In the final reports, descriptive elements increase, although the difference in this increase is not as great as the decrease in narrative elements mentioned above. There are more descriptive phrases scattered throughout the text. There are more "creative" complex NPs, that is, complex noun phrases which describe anatomic features encountered during the course of surgery. There are more agent incorporating NPs (i.e., complex NPs with lexical items indicating the agent's action), as well as more telegraphic reporting, in which modal verbs are not included in the sentences.

Finally, gaps in information that result from the reporting process and from the change in reporting styles were noted. Although examination of the loss of information from event to report was not the primary goal of the study, the above thick descriptions of the reporting processes demonstrate that using these methodologies for analysis can uncover sources of information loss. Suggestions were offered of ways to restructure certain talk in the operating room, and to change the format of the operative report to ensure a more complete reporting.

This study has used a number of methodological tools—ethnomethodological analysis, discourse analysis, and contrastive text analysis—to examine the process of text building in a medical setting from a linguistic point of view. Text building in this situation is a complex, yet generally untaught, process which is only now beginning to be reflected upon. Given the increasing role of the medical record in health care today, this study offers a series of vantage points from which the quality of medical record reporting can begin to be examined.

APPENDICES

APPENDIX A

Summary of Operation Recorded on Progress Notes Immediately Following Surgery

DATE	PROGRESS NOTES (please sign all entries)
4-1-84	**DIETETIC DEPT.** order received for Soft diet upon transfer, NPO → m/N 4/1/84 m — D.T
4/2/84	O.R. Note Pre-op dx - Cholecystitis Post-op dx - Same Operation - Cholecystectomy Surgeon: D. Assistant: Fluids - Crystalloid EBL - 20cc Drains None Complications - None Transferred to PAR in good condition.
4/2/84	Post Op ✓ Alert, oriented Afebrile, VSS Dressing intact s̄ drainage. Hsm·t voided yet → will cath for urine

APPENDIX B

Handwritten Summary of Operation Recorded on Progress Notes With Sketches

PROGRESS NOTES

Op Note: 9/15/81 5:00p.
Pre-op Dx: Gastric CA
Post-op Dx: Same
Procedure: Distal gastrectomy, Antecolic BII gastrojejunostomy, tube duodenostomy
Surgeon:
Assistants:
Anesthesia: General
Fluids: 4500 crystalloid, 1 U PRBC, 1 U whole blood
EBL: 650cc
Drains: duodenostomy tube, 2 penrose drains to RUQ
Complications: None
Findings: Large antral tumor mass 8 cm diam which extended into the pylorus & through the Jaboley pyloroplasty into the duodenum + also into the head of the pancrease. There were enlarged, hard sub-pyloric lymph nodes & there were hard tumor-like deposits extending along the hepato-duodenal ligamen to the porta hepatis.
Patient returned to PAR in stable condition.
Pyloroplasty Taken Down
& (Closed) (Difficult) over a Duodenostomy tube Drain

137

APPENDIX C

An Operative Report

DATE OF OPERATION: 4/2/84

SURGEON: Dr.

ASSISTANTS: Dr.
                                 W.S.U.-III

PREOPERATIVE DIAGNOSIS: Cholecystitis.

POSTOPERATIVE DIAGNOSIS: Cholecystitis.

OPERATION PERFORMED: Cholecystectomy.

ANESTHESIA: General.

INDICATIONS FOR SURGERY: Mrs.   is a 46-year-old white female who has had complaints of right upper quadrant pain, nausea and vomiting for the last year. A recent ultrasound showed cholelithiasis and she presents today for a cholecystectomy.

OPERATIVE TECHNIQUE: The patient was brought to the Operating Room and was placed in a supine position on the operating table. The abdomen was prepped and draped in the usual manner, after the Anesthesiology Department administered a general anesthetic. A seven inch incision extending from the xiphoid process below the costal margin was made. This was extended down through the subcutaneous tissue to the anterior rectus sheath. The anterior rectus sheath was incised. The rectus abdominis muscle was severed using cautery. The posterior rectus sheath was incised using a knife. The peritoneal cavity was then entered and the incision was extended medial and lateral with Metzenbaum scissors. Next the abdominal cavity was explored and there were no abnormalities noted, except adhesions to the anterior abdominal wall in the lower portion of the abdominal cavity. Next the gallbladder was isolated using packs in the superior portion below the liver to isolate the gallbladder. Next a Kocher was placed on the gallbladder and this was retracted so that the neck of the gallbladder could be seen. The cholecystoduodenal ligament was then incised and the base of the gallbladder was isolated. Next the cystic artery was dissected free and a #2-0 Vicryl suture was passed around the cystic artery. This was ligated and a second #2-0 Vicryl suture was placed again around the cystic artery. The artery was then ligated between these two sutures. Next the base of the gallbladder was dissected free using Metzenbaum scissors and cautery and the cystic duct was isolated using a right angle clamp. A #2-0 silk tie was placed around the cystic duct. Next the gallbladder was freed from the liver bed using blunt dissection and Metzenbaum scissors until the entire gallbladder was freed from the liver and attached to the common bile duct by the cystic duct. The cystic duct was then tied and ligated, allowing the gallbladder to be removed. The abdominal cavity was then irrigated with normal saline. Hemostasis was obtained and the abdominal wall was closed. First the posterior rectus sheath was closed using #2-0 Vicryl sutures. Then the anterior rectus sheath was closed using a #2-0 Vicryl

138

suture. The subcutaneous tissue was closed using #3-0 Vicryl and the
skin was closed using staples. No drains were left in. The patient
tolerated the procedure well. Preoperatively the patient had Cefoxitin,
one gram. Estimated blood loss: 20 cc. Fluids: Crystalloid.
Complications: None. The patient was transferred to the Post Anesthetic
Recovery Room in good condition.

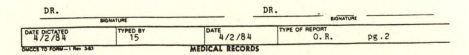

APPENDIX D

Preoperative Holding Record

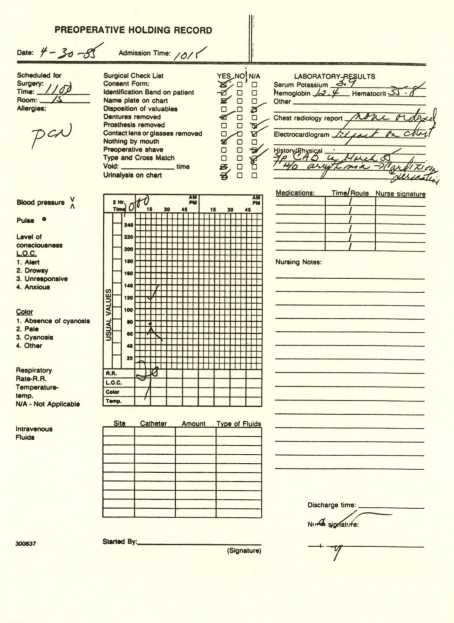

PREOPERATIVE HOLDING RECORD

Date: 4-30-85   Admission Time: 1015

Scheduled for Surgery:
Time: 1100
Room: 15
Allergies:

pcn

Surgical Check List	YES	NO	N/A
Consent Form:	☒	☐	☐
Identification Band on patient	☒	☐	☐
Name plate on chart	☒	☐	☐
Disposition of valuables	☐	☐	☒
Dentures removed	☒	☐	☐
Prosthesis removed	☐	☐	☒
Contact lens or glasses removed	☐	☐	☒
Nothing by mouth	☒	☐	☐
Preoperative shave	☐	☐	☒
Type and Cross Match	☐	☐	☒
Void: _____ time	☒	☐	☐
Urinalysis on chart	☒	☐	☐

LABORATORY RESULTS
Serum Potassium 3.9
Hemoglobin 12.4   Hematocrit 35.8
Other _____

Chest radiology report none ordered

Electrocardiogram report on chart

History/Physical
5p CAB in March 85
H/o arrythmia → Norpritron
                  Persantine

Blood pressure V Λ

Pulse •

Level of consciousness
L.O.C.
1. Alert
2. Drowsy
3. Unresponsive
4. Anxious

Color
1. Absence of cyanosis
2. Pale
3. Cyanosis
4. Other

Respiratory
Rate-R.R.
Temperature-temp.
N/A - Not Applicable

Intravenous Fluids

Medications: Time/Route   Nurse signature

Nursing Notes:

Site	Catheter	Amount	Type of Fluids

Discharge time: _____
Nurse signature:

300637

Started By: _____
(Signature)

Anesthesia Record

ANESTHESIA RECORD

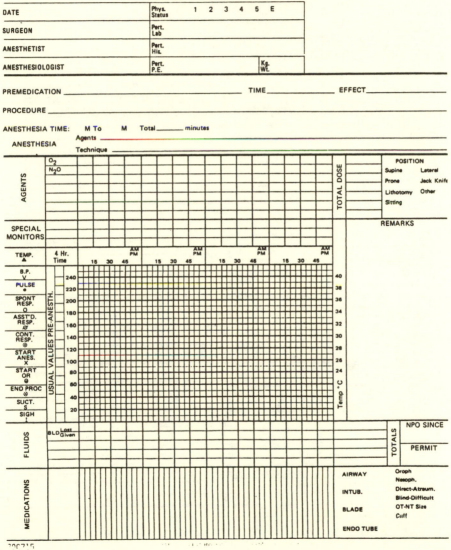

APPENDIX F

Surgical Record (Nurses)

SURGICAL RECORD

1	INPATIENT	DATE	
2	OUTPATIENT	ROOM NUMBER	
1	SCHEDULED CASE	CASE NUMBER	
2	ADD-ON CASE	ALLERGIES:	
3	EMERGENCY CASE		

AGE [ ]   SEX   M □   F □

ROOM ENTRY TIME	ANESTHESIA START TIME	SURGERY START TIME	SURGICAL POSITION:

ROOM EXIT TIME	ANESTHESIA END TIME	SURGERY END TIME

GROUND PLATE LOCATION: CAUTERY MACHINE NO.

WOUND CLASSIFICATION   SOLUTION: OPERATIVE PREP: □ YES □ NO
□ I □ I-P □ III □ IV   LENGTH OF TIME: MINUTES

PRE-OPERATIVE STATUS: □ AWAKE   DISCHARGED TO:
□ SLEEPING   □ DROWSY   □ ANXIOUS   □ PAR   □ NURSING FLOOR
□ UNRESPONSIVE   □ OTHER   □ ICU   □ HOME   □ OTHER

MICROSCOPE DRAPED: □ YES   □ NO   □ N/A

PRE-OPERATIVE:
DIAGNOSIS:

POST-OPERATIVE:
DIAGNOSIS:

PROCEDURE:		CODE
1.		
2.		
3.		
4.		

SURGEON:		CIRCULATING NURSE:	
ASSISTANT:		RELIEF:	
1.		1.	
2.		2.	
3.		3.	
ANESTHESIOLOGIST:		SCRUB NURSE:	
ANESTHETIST:		RELIEF:	
ANESTHESIA STUDENT:		1.	
OBSERVER:		2.	
		3.	

ANESTHESIA		DRUGS	CAST: □ YES □ NO
1	GENERAL		TYPE:
2	LOCAL/GENERAL		SPECIMENS: □ YES □ NO
3	SPINAL		
4	BLOCK:		
5	LOCAL		

IMPLANTS: □ YES □ NO   SIZE:
TYPE: MANUFACTURER:
SITE: LOT NUMBER:

PACKING: □ YES □ NO
TYPE: SITE:

DRAINS: □ YES □ NO   SIZE:
□ URINARY □ WOUND □ CHEST

OTHER: COMMENTS:

X-RAY: □ YES □ NO   SITE:

BLOOD TRANSFUSION: CULTURES: □ YES □ NO
□ YES □ NO   SITE:

POST-OPERATIVE INSTRUMENT COUNT: □ AEROBIC □ SLIDES
□ CORRECT □ INCORRECT □ N/A   □ ANAEROBIC □ WASHINGS

POST OPERATIVE SPONGE AND OTHER ITEM COUNT:

COUNT NO. 1.	COUNT NO. 2.	COUNT NO. 3.
SCRUB NURSE		
CIRCULATING NURSES SIGNATURE:		

White - PATIENT CHART   Green - OPERATING ROOM   Canary - MEDICAL RECORDS   Pink - DEPARTMENT OF SURGERY
300060 2/84

APPENDIX G

Post Anesthesia Recovery Record

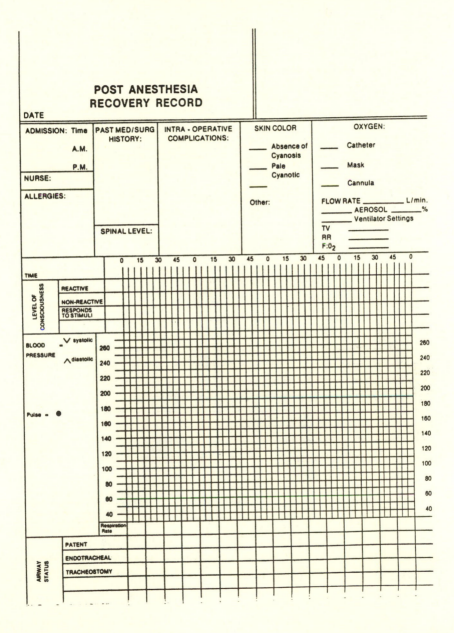

FLUIDS	IV SITE	ADMISSION CREDIT	DISCHARGE CREDIT	TOTAL	DRAINS	ADMISSION	DISCHARGE	TOTAL	DRESSINGS + LOCATION:
5% D/RL					Foley				
L.R.					Naso-Gastric				
									DRAINS: YES NO
Whole Blood									
Packed Cells									

TIME	MEDICATIONS		TYPE & LOCATION ROUTE	NURSE

NURSING PROGRESS NOTES

	DISCHARGE SUMMARY	DISCHARGE TIME	A.M. P.M.	PAR TIME ____ HRS ____ MIN.	NURSE:

Discharge Vital Signs	Condition	Skin Color	Dressing	Level of Consciousness	Airway Status
BP -	___ Satisfactory	___ Absence of	Condition:	___ Reactive	___ Patent
	___ Fair	Cyanosis		___ Non-reactive	___ Endotracheal
P -	___ Critical	___ Pale		___ Responds to	___ Tracheostomy
		___ Cyanotic		Stimuli	Other:
R -		___		Other:	

Report given to: By: M.D.A.

APPENDIX H

DICTATION OF OPERATIVE REPORT OF GASTROSTOMY AND CHOLECYSTECTOMY EXAMINED IN CHAPTER 2

1. This is Dr. _____ dictating the operative procedure/
2. of _____ (spells last name) number – – – – –/
3. Date of procedure five seven eighty four/
4. Preop diagnosis/
5. gastric mass/
6. Postop the *same*/
7. plus a porcelain gallbladder\
8. ah procedure exploratory laparotomy/
9. cholecystectomy/
10. and gastrostomy/
11. with excision of gastric mass\
12. Staff doctor _____/
13. *D* and assistant doctor _____\
14. Anesthesia general with endotracheal intubation\
15. hhhh this is a eighty year old black female/
16. who has had uh complaints of uh occasional mid epigastric pain/
17. and on physical exam has no palpable mass in her abdomen but
18. on uh but laboratory data has a CBC with chronic
19.   anemia\
20. hhhh she has been worked up uh within the last year which
21.   shows a colon with diverticular disease
22. and a stomach which has been scoped
23. and a CT scan which shows a *large mass* in the stomach
24.   starting up at the cardia\
25. on scope has previously been seen to have an ulceration
26.   in in the ah proposed site of bleeding\
27. hhh she's now agreeable to surgery and is taken for excision\
28.   of this mass which might possibly uh necessitate a
29.   gastrectomy\
30. hhhh she is laid in the supine position in the operating room/
31. general anesthesia administered with endotracheal intubation\
32. Foley is placed to dependant drainage/
33. and Levine tube is pl ah passed\
34. The abdomen is prepped and draped in the usual fashion/
35. and a uh midline incision is made from the xiphi
36.   ah down to just below the umbilicua/

37. ah using part of the previous ah
38. abdominal scar wh ich had been used for previous uh
39.   hysterectomy\
40. ah once through skin/
41. subcutaneous tissues/
42. linea alba and peritoneum/
43. the ah peritoneal – the abdominal cavity is entered/
44. and ah there are numerous adhesions which must be taken
45.   down sharply on either side of the abdomen for ah
46.   final freedom and adequate exploration\
47. this found (this) left lobe and right lobe of the liber
48.   are free of any ah masses or tumor\
49. The aorta is of normal size/
50. and no a aneurysmal dilatation of the vessels/
51. ah colon/
52. and intestinal structures seem to be without masses\
53. the ah stomach can be easily palpated and has a very
54.   *free*ly moveable
55. ah *base*ball ah size mass within its ah upper portion/
56. ah it does not penetrate through the wall of the stomach\
57. There are no (celiac) ah nodes/
58. and ah the gallbladder is ah (2.0) totally calcified and
59.   ah with stones\
60. ah (what is) first approached/
61. is the ah lesser sac which is opened/
62. and all of the greater curve taken to ah down between
63.   hemostats divided and tied with three oh *silk*/
64. ah the short gastric is left intact\
65. hhh once having accomplished this/
66. enough of the stomach was *freed up*
67. ah that ah two stay stutures of three oh vicryl could be
68. placed on the anterior *wall*/
69. with electrocautery a gastrotomy made\
70. the ah baseball sized mass is *eas*ily delivered into the
71.   ah into the wound/
72. and ah at its base and apices and base a three oh ah
73.   vicryl ah stay suture placed/
74. and with electrocautery the mass removed from its base\
75. ah resulting in a full thickness ah defect in the
76.   posterior wall of the stomach/
77. the mass itself is sent ah in toto to pathology for
78.   frozen section\
79. ah once ah having completed that\

80. the ah whatever bleedings at the base is controlled with
81.   a ah suture ligature of three oh vicryl/
82. the mucosa is closed with a running three oh vicryl
83. *and* from behind the wall interrupted three oh silk is
84.   placed completing a double layered closure of the
85.   posterior wall of the stomach\
86. the stay sutures are removed from inside of the stomach itself/
87. and the anterior gastrotomy is closed with three oh vicryl/
88. and the ah serosa of the stomach closed with interrupted
89.   three oh silk\
90. ah other stay sutures ah removed after that is completed\
91. hhhh once that is done/
92. the left upper quadrant examined for any further *bleeding*/
93. and packs left ah while the cholecystectomy is undertaken\
94. ah the ah *liver* is brought down into the operative field/
95. and the intestines ah packed away in the lower part of the
96.   abdomen/
97. and the gallbladder removed from its ah fundus/
98. down towards the < *background noise of squeaky door and
99.   talking> towards the ah portal ah structures with
100.   ah electrocautery and sharp dissection\
101. the cystic artery is identified/
102. ah clamped at a right angle/
103. divided and tied off with two oh silk\
104. we continue further on down with sharp dissection (to
105.   find) (and finding) (defining) our cystic duct/
106. and its entry into the common bile duct\
107. at this point this is *clamped*/
108. and the gallbladder divided off and removed and sent to
109.   Pathology\
110. the cystic duct itself being tied off with a ah free two
111.   oh silk uh tie\
112. ts having accomplished this/
113. this area is irrigated with normal *saline*/
114. examined for any sites of bleeding\
115. ah once having ah finished with that portion of the
116.   operation all packs are removed/
117. the ah gastrotomy site is reexamined
118. ah any bleeding left ah there in the abdominal wall is
119.   controlled wi electrocautery\
120. ah normal saline irrig*a*tion/
121. is ah done/
122. throughout the abdomen all four quadrants/

123. and ah then the midline of the abdomen is closed in *one*
124.   layer with interruped ah oh vicryl
125. the ah subcutaneous tissues are again irrigated with
126.   normal saline/
127. and the skin closed with ah staples\
128. dry dressing applied\
129. the *sponge* needle and instrument count were correct at
130.   the end of surgery/
131. the frozen section report on the mass in the stomach/
132. ah came back as a benign *prob*able leiomyoma/
133. and the patient tolerated the procedure very well and
134.   went to the recovery room in satisfactory condition\
135. this is doctor _____ dictating the operative procedure/
136. of (spells last name)\

thank you\.

APPENDIX I

RESEARCHER'S TRANSCRIPTION OF OPERATIVE REPORT OF CHOLECYSTECTOMY EXAMINED IN CHAPTER 3 (TEXT 1)

Indications: Mrs. _____ is a 46 year old white female who's had complaints of right upper quadrant pain, nausea, and vomiting for the last year. A recent ultrasound showed cholelithiasis and she presents today for cholecystectomy. *Operation:* The patient was brought to the operating room and placed in a supine position on the operating table. \/ The abdomen was prepped and draped in the usual manner after the anesthesiology department administered a general anesthetic. \/ A seven inch incision extending from the xiphoid process below the costal margin was made. This was extended down through the subcutaneous tissue to the anterior rectal sheath. The anterior rectal sheath was incised. The rectus abdominis muscle was severed using a cautery and the posterior rectus sheath was incised using a knife. The peritoneal cavity was then entered. \/ The incision was extended medial and lateral with Metzenbaum scissors. Next the abdominal cavity was explored and there were no abnormalities noted except adhesion to the anterior abdominal wall on the lower portion of the abdominal cavity. \/ Next the gallbladder was isolated using packs in the inferior portion below the liver to isolate the gallbladder. Next the Kocher was placed on the gallbladder and this was retracted so that the neck of the gallbladder could be seen. The cholecystoduodenal ligament was then incised and the base of the gallbladder was isolated. Next the cystic artery was dissected free and a 2-0 vicryl suture was placed again around the cystic artery. This was ligated and a second 2-0 vicryl suture was placed again around the cystic artery. The artery was then ligated between the two sutures. \/ Next the base of the gallbladder was dissected free using Metzenbaum scissors and cautery and the cystic duct was isolated using a right angle clamp. A 2-0 silk tie was placed around the cystic duct. \/ Next the gallbladder was freed from the liver bed using blunt dissection and Metzenbaum scissors until the entire gallbladder was free from the liver and attached to the common bile duct by the cystic duct. The cystic duct was then tied and then the cystic duct was ligated allowing the gallbladder to be removed. \/ The abdominal cavity was then irrigated using normal saline. Hemostasis was obtained and the abdominal was closed. Then the anterior rectus sheath was closed using 2-0 vicryl suture. The subcutaneous tissue was closed using 3-0 vicryl and the skin was closed using staples. \/ No drains were left in. The patient tolerated the procedure well. Preoperatively the patient had Cephoxytan 1 gram. Estimated blood loss 20 ccs. Fluids crystalloid. Complications none. The patient was transferred to PAR in good condition.

APPENDIX J

LINQUISTICALLY SENSITIVE TRANSCRIPTION OF OPERATIVE REPORT EXAMINED IN CHAPTER 3 (TEXT 2)

[1] _____

Operation   The patient was brought to the operating room and placed in a supine position on the operating table

[2] _____

(3.0)   The abdomen

(2.0)   was prepped and draped in the usual manner

        (.)   after the anesthesiology department administered a general anesthetic

[3] _____

(3.0)   a

(2.0)   seven inch incision extending

        (.)   from the xiphoid process

        (.)   below the costal margin

(1.0)   was made. This was extended down through the

        (.)   subcutaneous tissue

        (.)   to the anterior rectal sheath. The anterior rectal sheath was incised

        (.)   the

(2.0)   rectus abdominis muscle was severed using a

(2.0)   cautery

        (.)   and the posterior rectus sheath was incised using

        (.)   a knife. The peritoneal cavity was then entered.

[4] _____

        The incision was extended

        (.)   medial and lateral with

(1.0)   Metzenbaum scissors.

(3.0)   Next the abdominal cavity was explored

        (.)   and there were no abnormalities noted except

        (.)   adhesion to the anterior abdominal wall on the lower

        (.)   portion of the abdominal cavity.

[5] _____

(4.0)   Next the gallbladder was isolated using

        (.)   packs in the

(3.0)   inferior portion

        (.)   below the liver to isolate the gallbladder.

(11.1) Next the Kocher was placed on the gallbladder and this was retracted

(.)   so that the neck of the gallbladder could be seen. The

(.)   cholecystoduodenal ligament was then incised and the base of the gallbladder was

(.)   isolated.

[6a] _____

(2.0)   Next the cystic artery was dissected

(.)   free and a

[6b] _____

(2.0)   2-0 vicryl suture was passed around the cystic artery. This was

(.)   ligated and a second 2-0 vicryl suture was placed again around the

(2.0)   cystic artery. The artery was then

(.)   ligated between the

(2.0)   two sutures.

[7a] _____

(3.0)   Next the base of the gallbladder

(.)   was dissected free using Metzenbaum scissors and cautery.

[7b] _____

(4.0)   and the cystic duct was

(.)   ligated – the cystic duct was isolated using

(.)   a right angle

(2.0)   clamp. A

[7c] _____

(1.0)   2-0

(.)   silk tie was placed around the

(2.0)   cystic duct.

[8] _____

(9.0)   Next the gallbladder was

(.)   freed from the

(2.0)   liver bed using blunt dissection and Metzenbaum scissors until the entire gallbladder was free from the

(.)   liver and attached to the

(2.0)   common bile duct by the cystic ar– cystic duct.

[9] _____

(2.0)   The cystic duct was then

(1.0)   tied and the gallbladder was –

(1.0)   and then the cystic duct was

(3.0)   ligated removing the – allowing the gallbladder to be removed.

[10] _____

(5.0)   The

(.)   abdominal cavity was then irrigated

(.)   using normal saline.

[10b] _____

(2.0)   Hemostasis was obtained

[10c]   _____

(1.0)   and the abdominal wall was closed.

       (.)   First the posterior rectus sheath was closed using

(1.0)   2–0 vicryl

       (.)   suture

[10d]   _____

(2.0)   Then the

       (.)   anterior rectus sheath was

(2.0)   closed using 2–0 vicryl suture

[10e]   _____

(2.0)   The subcutaneous tissue was

       (.)   closed using 3–0

       (.)   vicryl and the skin was closed using staples.

[11]   _____

       (.)   No drains were left in. The patient tolerated the procedure well.

       (.)   preoperatively the patient had

[11b]   _____

(2.0)   Cephoxytan one gram

[11c]   _____

(1.0)   Estimated blood loss

       (.)   20ccs. Fluids crystalloid. Complications none.

       The patient was transferred to PAR in good condition.

       Dr. _____ finishing a discharge summary

       /er and OR dictation on _____ Thank you.

APPENDIX K

TEXT DIVIDED ACCORDING TO EPISODES AS NOTED BY RESIDENT IN CHAPTER3 (TEXT 3)

Episode 1

"The beginning indicates the patient was brought into the operating room."

Operation: The patient was brought to the operating room and placed in a supine position on the operating table

Episode 2

"and then the next step was prepping and draping the patient"

(3.0)   the abdomen
(2.0)   was prepped and drapped in the usual manner
        (.)   after the anesthesiology department administered a general anesthetic

Episode 3

"then making the incision and getting into the abdominal cavity was the next step"

(3.0)   a
(2.0)   seven inch incision extending
        (.)   from the xiphoid process
        (.)   below the costal margin
(1.0)   was made. This was extended down through the
        (.)   subcutaneous tissue
        (.)   to the anterior rectal sheath. The anterior rectal sheath was
incised
        (.)   the
(2.0)   rectus abdominis muscle was severed using a
(2.0)   cautery
        (.)   and the posterior rectus sheath was incised using
        (.)   a knife. The peritoneal cavity was *then* entered

Episode 4

"then exploration − exploration of the abdominal cavity"

                                        The incision was extended
        (.)   medial and lateral with
(1.0)   Metzenbaum scissors.
(3.0)   *next* the abdominal cavity was explored

(.)   and there were no abnormalities noted except
(.)   adhesion to the anterior abdominal wall on the lower
(.)   portion of the abdominal cavity

Episode 5

"and then starting with the bulk of the operation; isolating the gallbladder"

(4.0)   *Next* the gallbladder was isolated using
    (.)   packs in the
(3.0)   inferior portion
    (.)   below the liver to isolate the gallbladder
(11.1) *Next* the Kocher was placed on the gallbladder and this was retracted
    (.)   so that the neck of the gallbladder could be seen the
    (.)   cholecystoduodenal ligament was then incised and the base of
the gallbladder was
    (.)   isolated

Episode 6

"and then isolating the cystic artery"

6–A
(2.0)   *Next* the cystic artery was dissected
    (.)   free and a
6–B
(2.0)   2–0 vicryl suture was passed around the cystic artery this was
    (.)   ligated and a second 2–0 vicryl suture was placed again around
the
(2.0)   cystic artery
6–C
                     the artery was then
    (.)   ligated between the
(2.0)   two sutures

Episode 7

"then isolating the cystic duct and tying that"

7–A
(3.0)   *Next* the base of the gallbladder
    (.)   was dissected free using Metzenbaum scissors and cautery
7–B
(4.0)   and the cystic duct was
    (.)   ligated — the cystic duct was isolated using
    (.)   a right angle
(2.0)   clamp
7–C

A
(1.0) 2–0
     (.) silk tie was placed around the
(2.0) cystic duct

Episode 8

"and then removing the gallbladder from the liver bed"

(9.0) *Next* the gallbladder was
     (.) freed from the
(2.0) liver bed using blunt dissection and Metzenbaum scissors until the
entire gallbladder was free from the
     (.) liver and attached to the
(2.0) common bile duct by the cystic ar – cystic duct

Episode 9

"and then finally tying the cystic duct"

(2.0) the cystic duct was *then*
(1.0) tied and the gallbladder was
(1.0) and *then* the cystic duct was
(3.0) ligated removing the allowing the gallbladder to be removed

Episode 10

"and then basically the rest of it was closing the abdominal cavity"

10–A
(5.0) the
     (.) abdominal cavity was then irrigated
     (.) using normal saline
10–B
(2.0) Hemostasis was obtained
10–C
(1.0) and the abdominal wall was closed
     (.) first the posterior rectus sheath was closed using
(1.0) 2–0 vicryl
     (.) suture
10–D
(2.0) *then* the
     (.) anterior rectus sheath was
(2.0) closed using 2–0 vicryl suture
10–E
(2.0) the subcutaneous tissue was
     (.) closed using 3–0
     (.) vicryl and the skin was closed using staples

Episode 11

"and then a little bit of the postop course and a summary of some of the important statistics like the blood loss and the fluids and what condition the patient was in when she left the room."

11-A
     (.) no drains were left in the patient tolerated the procedure well
11-B
     (.) preoperatively the patient had
(2.0) Cephoxytan one gram
11-C
(1.0) estimated blood loss
     (.) 20 ccs. fluids crystalloid complications none the patient was transferred to PAR in good condition

BIBLIOGRAPHY

Becker, A. L. 1980. Text-Building, Epistemology, and Aesthetics in Javanese Shadow Theatre. In Becker and A. Yengoyan, eds. *The Imagination of Reality*. Norwood, N.J., Ablex.

Beckman, H. B. and R. M. Frankel. 1984. The Effect of Physician Behavior on the Collection of Data. *Annals of Internal Medicine* 101:5:692–696.

Bernhardt, S. 1981. Text Structure and Rhetoric in Scientific Prose. Unpublished Ph.D. Dissertation, University of Michigan.

Black, J. B. and G. H. Bower. 1979. Episodes as Chunks in Narrative Memory. *Journal of Verbal Learning and Verbal Behavior* 18:309–318.

Bley-Vroman, R. and L. Selinker. 1984. Research Design in Rhetorical/ Grammatical Studies: A Proposed Optimal Research Strategy. *English for Specific Purposes* 82–84:1–6.

Bross, I. D. J., R. L. Priore, P. A. Shapiro, D. F. Stermole, and B. B. Anderson. 1969. Feasibility of Automated Information systems in the Users' Natural Language. *American Scientist* 57:2:193–205.

_____., P. A. Shapiro, and B. B. Anderson. 1972. How Information is Carried in Scientific Sub-Languages. *Science* 176:4041:1303–7.

Brown, G. and G. Yule. 1983. *Discourse Analysis*. Cambridge, England, Cambridge University Press.

Bruce, N. J. 1984. Rhetorical Constraints and Information Structure in Medical Research Report Writing. *EP Newsletter: English for Medical and Paramedical Purposes*. Safat, Kuwait, Medical Skills Division, Health Sciences Centre, Kuwait University.

Card, W. I., W. Sircus, and A. N. Smith. 1979. Evidental Value of the Hospital Record in Clinical Decision Making. *British Medical Journal* 1:6174:1305–8.

Chafe, W. 1979. The Flow of Thought and the Flow of Language. In Givon, ed.

Chafe, W. 1980. The Deployment of Consciousness in the Production of a Narrative. In Chafe, ed. *The Pear Stories: Cognitive, Cultural, and Linguistic Aspects of Narrative Productioin*. Norwood, N.J., Ablex.

Charfoos, L. S. 1974. *The Medical Malpractice Case: A Complete Handbook*. Englewood Cliffs, N.J., Prentice-Hall.

Cherkin, D. C., W. R. Phillips, and W. R. Gillanders. 1984. Assessing the Reliability of Data from Patient Medical Records. *Journal of Family Practice* 18:6:937–940.

Cicourel, A. V. 1974. Interviewing and Memory. In C. Cherry, ed. *Pragmatic Aspects of Human Communication*. Dordrecht, Holland, D. Reidel.

Cicourel, A. V. 1975. Discourse and Text: Cognitive and Linguistic Processes in Studies of Social Structure. *Versus* 12:2:33–84.

Cofer, J. 1985. Legislative Currents. *Journal of the American Medical Record Association* 56:4:23, 49.

Cooper, J. KI., ed. 1978. *Medical Malpractice Claims*. Washington, D.C., U.S. Department H.E.W.

Courch, N.P., N.L. Tilney, A. A. Rayner, and F. D. Moore. 1981. The High Cost of Low-Frequency Events: The Anatomy and Economics of Surgical Mishaps. *New England Journal of Medicine* 304:11:634–637.

Currie, M. S. 1985. Clinical Data Quality: Impact on Revenue. *Journal of the American Medical Record Association* 56:4:25–31.

de Groot, Adriaan. 1965. *Thought and Choice in Chess*. The Hague, Mouton.

Di Pietro, R. J., ed. 1982. *Linguistics and the Professions: Proceedings of the Second Annual Delaware Symposium on Language Studies*. Norwood, N.J., Ablex.

Donabedian, A. 1966. Evaluating the Quality of Medical Care. *Milbank Memorial Fund Quarterly* 44:3:166–203.

Douglas, D. and C. Pettinari. 1983. Grounded Ethnography: A Method Adaptable to the Production of Communicative ESP Materials. Toronto, TESOL Conference, March 18, 1983.

Drew, E. 1984. A Political Journal. *The New Yorker*. October 29, 1984:130–157.

DuBois, B. L. 1981. The Construction of Noun Phrases in Biomedical Journal Articles. In J. Hoedt et al., eds. *Pragmatics and LSP*. Copenhagen, UNESCO ALSED LSP Network and Copenhagen School of Economics.

Dudley, H., C. Rob, and R. Smith, eds. 1977. *Operative Surgery: Fundamental International Techniques*. London, Butterworths.

Eiler, M. A. 1983. Meaning and Choice in Writing about Literature. In Fine and Freedle, eds.

Ficarra, B. J. 1968. *Surgical and Allied Malpractice,* Springfield, IL, Charles C. Thomas.

Fessel, W. J. and E. E. Van Brunt. 1972. Assessing Quality of Care from the Medical Record. *New England Journal of Medicine* 284:3:134–138.

Fillmore, C. J. 1968. The Case for Case. In E. Bach and R. Harms, eds. *Universals in Linguistic Theory*. New York, Holt, Rinehart and Winston.

Fine, J. and R. O. Freedle, eds. 1983. *Developmental Issues in Discourse*. Norwood, N.J. Ablex.

Flower, L. 1981. *Problem Solving Strategies for Writing*. New York, Harcourt Brace Jovanovich.

Foucault, M. 1973. *The Birth of the Clinic: An Archaeology of Medical Perception*. New York, Vintage Books.

Frankel, R. 1981. Record Keeping in the Context of Communicative Interaction. Paper presented at the University of Michigan Department of Communication. October 26, 1981.

Frankel, R. 1985. "Captain I Was Trying to Bring Up the Fact that You Made a Mistake Earlier:" Deference and Demeanor at 30,000 Feet. *Proceedings of the Third Annual International Symposium on Aviation Psychology.* Columbus, Ohio State University.

Frankel, R. In press. The Medical Record and the Social Construction of Clinical Reality. *Language at Work: Studies in Situated Interaction.* R. Frankel, ed. Norwood, N.J. Ablex.

Garfinkel, H. 1967. "Good" Organizational Reasons for "Bad" Clinic Records. In H. Garfinkel, ed. *Studies in Ethnomethodology.* Englewood Cliffs, N.J., Prentice-Hall.

Geertz, C. 1973. *The Interpretation of Cultures.* New York, Basic Books, Inc.

Gilbert, G. N. and M. Mulkay. 1984. *Opening Pandora's Box: A Sociological Analysis of Scientists' Discourse.* Cambridge, England, Cambridge University Press.

Givon, T., ed. 1979. *Syntax and Semantics 12: Discourse and Syntax.* New York, Academic Press.

Givon, T. 1983. Topic Continuity in Discourse: A Quantitative Cross-Language Study. In T. Givon, ed., *Typological Studies in Language.* Amsterdam, T. Benjamins.

Goffman, E. 1959. *The Presentation of Self in Everyday Life.* Garden City, N.Y., Doubleday Anchor Books.

Goffman, E. 1981. *Forms of Talk.* Philadelphia, University of Pennsylvania Press.

Goguen, J. A. and C. Linde. 1983. Linguistic Methodology for the Analysis of Aviation Accidents. Technical Report, National Aeronautics and Space Administration. NASA Contractor Report 3741.

Goldstone, J. and L. W. Way. 1976. The Use of Medical Audits in Surgical Education. *Surgery* 84:25–32.

Good Medical Records Can Be Strongest Malpractice Defense. 1983. *Michigan Medicine* 82:3:6–10.

Gregory, D. R. 1982. Medical Malpractice Prevention. In C. H. Wecht, ed. *Legal Medicine 1982.* Philadelphia, W. B. Saunders.

Hakuta, K. 1974. Prefabricated Patterns and the Emergence of Structure in Second Language Acquisition. *Lanaguage Learning* 24:287–297.

Harris, E. 1983. A Theoretical Perspective on "How To" Discourse. In P. V. Anderson, R. J. Brockmann, and C. R. Miller, eds. *New Essays in Technical and Scientific Communication: Research, Theory, Practice.* Farmingdale, N. Y., Baywood Publishing Company.

Harris, Z. 1968. *Mathematical Structures of Language.* New York, Interscience.

Hinds, J. 1979. Organizational Patterns in Discourse. In Givon, ed.

Hofstadter, D. 1979. *Godel, Escher, Bach: An Eternal Golden Braid.* New York, Vintage Books.

Horwitz, R. I. and E. C. Yu. 1984. Assessing the Reliability of Epidemiologic Data Obtained from Medical Records. *Journal of Chronic Diseases* 37:11:825–831.

Huckin, T. and L. Olsen. 1983. On the Use of Informants in LSP Discourse

Analysis. In A. K. Pugh and J. M. Ulijn, eds. *Reading for Professional Purposes: Studies in Native and Foreign Languages.* London, Heinemann.

Huffman, E. K. 1981. *Medical Records Management.* Revised 7th ed. Berwyn, IL, Physicians' Record Company.

Jesperson, O. 1964. *Essentials of English Grammar.* University, AL, University of Alabama Press.

Johnson, I. C., S. L. Tsao, I. D. J. Bross, D. P. Shedd. 1979. Natural Language and a Computer System in Medical Records. *Methods of Information in Medicine* 18:1:15–17.

Johnson-Laird, P. 1983. *Mental Models: Towards a Cognitive Science of Lnaguage, Inference, and Consciousness.* Cambridge, Cambridge University Press.

Joint Commission on Accreditation of Hospitals. 1981. *Making QA Work for You!* Chicago, JCAH.

Kerr, A. S. 1983. Malpractice Case Histories: Large Percentage of Malpractice Cases Begin Right on the Medical Records. *Michigan Medicine* 82:4:99.

Kloss, L. 1985. Executive Message: Who Really Is in Charge? *Journal of the American Medical Record Association* 56:5:14–15.

Knorr, K. and D. Knorr. 1978. From Scenes to Scripts: On the Relationship between Laboratory Research and Published Paper in Science. Research Memorandum No. 132. Vienna, Austria, Institute for Advanced Studies.

Knorr-Cetina, K. 1981. *The Manufacture of Knowledge: An Essay on the Constructivist and Contextual Nature of Science.* New York, Pergamon.

Korcok, M. 1977. When the Lawyer is Called In Your Best Friend is a Good Set of Records. *Canadian Medical Association Journal* 116:6:687–690.

Kramarae, C. 1981. *Women and Men Speaking: Frameworks for Analysis.* Rowley, MA, Newbury House.

Kurland, L. T. and C. A. Molgaard. 1981. The Patient Record in Epidemiology. *Scientific American* 245:4:54–63.

Labov, W. 1972. The Transformation of Experience in Narrative Syntax. In *Language in the Inner City.* Philadelphia, University of Pennsylvania Press.

Labov, W. and D. Fanshel. 1977 *Therapeutic Discourse: Psychotherapy as Conversation.* New York, Academic Press.

Labov, W. and J. Waltezky. 1967. Narrative Analysis. In *Essays on the Verbal and Visual Arts.* Seattle, University of Washington Press.

Lackstrom, J., L. Selinker, and L. Trimble. 1973. Technical Rhetorical Principles and Grammatical Choice. *TESOL Quarterly* 7:2:127–316.

Latour, B. and S. Woolgar. 1979. *Laboratory Life: The Social Construction of Scientific Facts.* Beverly Hills, CA, Sage Publications.

Lee, S. P. 1983. The Stomach after Cholecystectomy. *The American Journal of Surgeryf* 146:325–326.

Levinson, S. 1979. Activity Types and Language. *Linguistics* 17:365;-399.

Linde, C. 1983. A Framework for Formal Models of Discourse: What We Can Model and Why. *Text* 3:3:271–276.

Linde, C. and J. Goguen. 1978. Structure of Planning Discourse. *Journal of Social Biological Structures* 1:219–251.

Longacre, R. E. 1976. An Anatomy of Speech Notions. Lisse, Peter de Ridder.

Longacre, R. E. 1979. The Paragraph as a Grammatical Unit. In Givon, ed.

Lynch, M. E. 1979. Art and Artifact in Laboratory Science: A Study of Shop Work and Shop Talk in a Research Laboratory. Unpublished Ph.D. Dissertation. University of California, Irvine.

Lyons, T. and B. Payne. 1974. Relationship of Physicians' Medical Recording Performance to Medical Care Performance. *Medical Care* 5:713–20.

Martin, J. R. 1983. The Development of Register. In Fine and Freedle, eds.

Mathes, J. C. and D. W. Stevenson. 1976. *Designing Technical Reports: Writing for Audiences in Organizations.* Indianapolis, Bobbs-Merrill Educational Publishing.

Matte, P. J. 1971. Legal Implications of the Patient's Medical Record. In C. H. Wecht, ed. *Legal Medicine Annual 1971.* New York, Meredith Corporation.

Mehnert, T. 1985. The Reassessment Process: Key to a Meaningful Quality Assurance Program. *QRB* 11:4:127–131.

Morgan, E. 1980. *The Making of a Woman Surgeon.* New York, Berkeley Books.

New York Times. Letting Panels Decide the Fate of Defective Infants. January 12, 1984.

Newtson, D. 1973. Attribution and The Unit of Perception of Ongoing Behavior. *Journal of Personality and Social Psychology* 28:28–38.

Newtson, D. and G. Engquist. 1976. The Perceptual Organization of Ongoing Behavior. *Journal of Experimental Social Psychology* 12:436–450.

Newtson, D., G. Engquist, and J. Bois. 1977. The Objective Basis of Behavior Units. *Journal of Personality and Social Psychology* 35:12:847–861.

Paget, M. 1983. Experience and Knowledge. *Human Studies* 6:67–90.

Payne, B. C. 1979. The Medical Record as a Basis for Assessing Physician Competence. *Annals of Internal Medicine* 91:623–629.

Pettinari, C. 1983. The Function of a Grammatical Alternation in Fourteen Surgical Reports. *Applied Linguistics* 4:1:55–76.

Pettinari, C. 1985. A Comparison of the Production of Surgical Reports by Native and Nonnative Speaking Surgeons. J. D. Benson and W. S. Greaves, eds. *Selected Applied Papers from the Ninth International Systemic Workshop.* Norwood, N.J., Ablex.

Prince, E., J. Frader and C. Bosk. 1982. On Hedging in Physician-Physician Discourse. In R. Di Pietro, ed.

Quirk, R. and S. Greenbaum. 1973. *A Concise Grammar of Contemporary English.* New York, Harcourt, Brace, Jovanovich.

Raffel, S. 1979. *Matters of Fact: A Sociological Inquiry.* London, Rutledge & Kegan Paul.

Roberts, J. S. and R. M. Walczak. 1984. Toward Effective Quality Assurance: The Evolution and Current Status of the JCAH QA Standard. *QRB* 10:1:11–15.

Rozovsky, L. E. 1978. Medical Records as Evidence. *Dimensions in Health Services* 55:7:16–17.

Rumelhart, D. 1975. Notes on a Schema for Stories. D. Bobrow and A. Collins, eds. *Representation and Understanding: Studies in Cognitive Science.* New York, Academic Press.

Sager, N., I. D. J. Bross, G. Story, P. Bastedo, E. Marsh and D. Shedd. 1982. Automatic Encoding of Clinical Narrative. *Computers in Biology and Medicine* 12:1:43–55.

Schank, R. C. and R. P. Abelson . 1977. *Scripts, Plans, Goals and Understanding: An Inquiry into Human Knowledge Structures.* Hillsdale, NJ, Lawrence Erlbaum.

Schenkein, J., ed. 1978. *Studies in the Organization of Conversational Interaction.* New York, Academic Press.

Selinker, L. 1979. On the Use of Informants in Discourse Analysis and 'Language for Specialized Purposes.' *International Review of Applied Linguistics* 17:3:189–215.

Serluco, R. J. and K. Johnson. 1983. Importance of the Medical Record Process in a DRG-Based System. *QRB* 9:9:268–272.

Shapiro, P. A. 1967. ACORN: An Automatic Coder of Report Narrative. *Methods of Information Management* 6:189–215.

Skillicorn, S. A. 1981. Improved Quality Controls in Hospitals: A Necessity. The *Journal of Legal Medicine* 2:4:471–489.

Squire, S. 1985. The Doctors' Dilemma: Practicing Defensive Medicine. *New York* 18:11:54–62.

Stanley-Brown, E. G. 1983. How to Dictate Operative Notes. *Resident and Staff Physician,* pp. 109–110.

Swale, J. 1986. Genre Based Analysis to Language Across the Curriculum. In T. Llamzon, ed. *Language Across the Curriculum.* 1985 RELC Seminar Proceedings. pp. 10 − 22.

Taber, C. W. 1962. Taber's Cyclopedic Medical Dictionary. Ninth edition. Philadelphia, F. A. Davis Company.

Tannen, D. ed. 1982. *Georgetown University Round Table on Languages and Linguistics 1981. Analyzing Discourse: Text and Talk.* Washington, D.C., Georgetown University Press.

Tannen, D. and C. Wallat. 1982. A Sociolinguistic Analysis of Multiple Demands on the Pediatrician in Doctor/Mother/Child Interaction. In R. Di Pietro, ed.

Tomlin, R. and R. Rhodes. 1979. An Introduction to Information Distribution in Ojibwa. *CLS* 15:307–20.

Treichler, P., R. Frankel, C. Kramerae, K. Zoppi, and H. Beckman. 1984. Problems and Problems: Power Relationships in the Medical Encounter. In C. Kramerae, M. Schultz, and W. O'Barr, eds. *Language and Power.* Beverly Hills, Sage Publications.

van Dijk, Teun. 1982. Episodes as Units of Discourse Analysis. In Tannen, ed.

van Naerssen, M. 1985. Medical Records: One Variation of Physicians' Language. *International Journal of the Sociology of Language.* 51:43–73.

Wagner, B. M. 1984. The Surgical Pathology Report. *Human Pathology* 15:1.

Warner, A. M. 1985. Education for Roles and Responsibilities in Quality Assurance: Physician Leadership. *QRB* 11:4:111–114.

Weed, L. 1971. *Medical Records, Medical Education and Patient Care.* Cleveland, The Press of Case Western Reserve.

Wittgenstein, L. 1958. *Philosophical Investigations.* New York, MacMillan.

Zaslow, J. 1978. What is Malpractice in General Surgery? In. C. H. Hecht, ed. *Legal Medicine Annual 1978.* New York, Appleton-Century-Crofts.

AUTHOR INDEX

SUBJECT INDEX